mindful beads

mindful beads

20 inspiring ideas for stringing and personalizing your own mala and prayer beads, plus their meanings

Alice Peck

CICO BOOKS

LONDON NEW YORK

For Duane and Tyl

Published in 2018 by CICO Books
An imprint of Ryland Peters & Small Ltd
20–21 Jockey's Fields   341 E 116th St
London WC1R 4BW   New York, NY 10029

www.rylandpeters.com

10 9 8 7 6 5 4 3 2 1

A CIP catalog record for this book is available from
the Library of Congress and the British Library.

ISBN: 978-1-78249-561-1

Printed in China

Editor: Marion Paull
Designer: Emily Breen
Photographer: Joanna Henderson
Stylist: Luis Peral
Illustrator: Stephen Dew (artworks on
pages 103–104 by Melissa Launay)

Commissioning editor: Kristine Pidkameny
Senior editor: Carmel Edmonds
Art director: Sally Powell
Production controller: Mai-Ling Collyer
Publishing manager: Penny Craig
Publisher: Cindy Richards

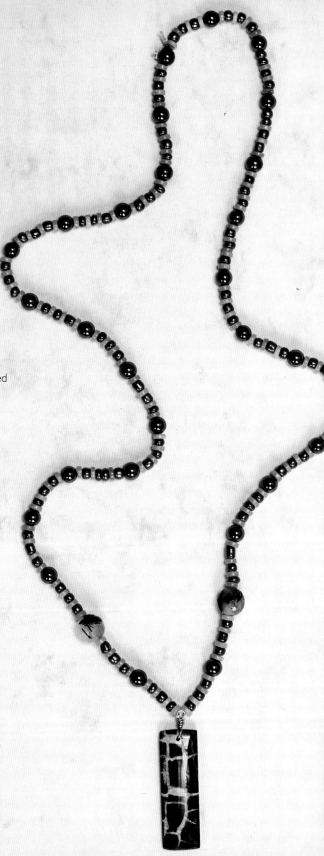

contents

"Sweet present of the present."

introduction

I am neither jeweler nor an expert on beads, but I do like to think about how to find the sacred in the everyday things that touch our lives and use this experience to arrive at a place of mindfulness. That is why I wrote this book, to explore the process of creating something—strands of beads—and imbuing that process with significance and perhaps a deeper, even spiritual, purpose.

Mindfulness for me means being awake and connected to every moment, as the twentieth-century French poet Jacques Prévert wrote in "Alicante," receiving the "*Doux présent de la présent*" or "Sweet present of the present." Mindfulness is a practice of contemplation that forms the basis for most meditation and prayer in that it is a way to learn to strengthen and control attention. It is especially beneficial when done with positive and even altruistic intent.

The English word "bead" is derived from Middle English *bede*, meaning "prayer." Throughout history, strings of beads have been common to all peoples, devotions, and beliefs. They are called by many names—mala, rosary, misbahah, komboloi, prayer beads—but no matter the culture or context, they are a tangible symbol of connection to our memories, our hopes, our loves, our gratitude, gods, and our best selves. Beads can tell a story, and be personal reminders or public declarations. They can inspire us, help us to celebrate a person, thing, or feeling we love, or ground us as we work through a difficulty.

Beads are as old as humanity. Archaeologists discovered ancient Egyptian beads made of meteoric iron in 3200 BCE, two thousand years before the

Iron Age! Perforated seashells used as beads found in Ksar Akil, north of Beirut, Lebanon are between 41,000 and 35,000 years old. Beads discovered in the Indus Valley date to 2000 BCE. People have strung pieces of shell and seeds since time immemorial and very soon thereafter began to imbue them with meaning.

And yet, they are as modern as a click on the Internet from where beads of any imaginable material are more easily acquired than ever before. They can be crafted from rosewood, clay, amber, lapis, coins, diamonds, glass, metal, plastic, pebbles, gems, buttons, paper, Lucite, nuts, crystal, flower petals, acorns, pearls, eggshells, bobbins, eucalyptus pods, faience, sharks' teeth, pasta, yak bones, wood, braided grass, snake vertebrae …

As you will see in this book, the connotations of beads are as varied as the materials. It is not so much what you string as why and how you string it—with mindful intent. There is symbolism in the type, number, and source of the beads and the words that go with them—mantras, prayers, promises, affirmations, and meditations. For example, 108 is a sacred number in Hinduism and yoga, and eight is associated with resurrection and new beginnings in the Christian Bible. Date pits from Mecca or berries picked along pilgrimages or at holy sites are permeated with the meaning of the place. Since beads are almost always strung in a circle, the form and all that implies—continuity, interconnection, the infinite—matters and has significance as well.

Each chapter of this book includes three parts. First, a description of the beads within the context of history, lore, traditional uses, and materials. Then comes "creation," the hands-on or how-to element, including types of

beads, different ways to make or acquire them, special numbers or knots, colors, or symbolism. Examples, suggestions, or patterns are included for each project. Lastly, in "consideration," I offer ways of practicing with, and connecting to, the beads' meanings and using them in rituals, meditation, mantras, incantations, offerings, asanas, and visualizations. The idea is to make them matter within your life, to help you find the Divine in the day-to-day.

In this book, we will explore all of this and go further, as we learn where to find and how to make beads, instill them with significance, and incorporate that thought, protection, and presence into our lives. Mindful beads are more than an ornament. They are a way to keep the sacred close to our hearts and hands. They are symbols, of growth, spirituality, belief, and promise.

the long and the short of it
STRINGING BEADS

Before we begin to work mindfully with beads, there are a few things to know. What follows is some general information about how to string beads in long and short strands, useful knots and gadgets, and the supplies you'll need, as well as types of beads. Notes on sources appear at the end of the book. I have tried to keep the instructions here and throughout the book as simple as possible, because mindful beading is more about the process of creating the strands—being present, intentional, meditative—than a specific technique or product. Approach this book more as a guide to following your bliss (as mythologist and writer Joseph Campbell famously recommended) than as a guide to following the rules.

it all starts with a string ...

* The thickness depends on the beads you choose but in general it is best to go for something between 0.7 mm and 1 mm. Gauge your string to the beads—the lighter the beads the finer the thread, heavier beads need something sturdier.

* The most important thing is to use a string that can survive an accidental dip in the ocean or the bathtub so that it won't deteriorate or rot. It can be nylon filament, polyester, silk, wire, lanyard, or a thin chain.

* For longer strands of beads I prefer 100% silk thread cord, which comes in an abundance of colors and can be bought with the needle already (handily) threaded. You can get it in two- or three-strand gauges depending on the weight of your beads. It's strong and knots easily.

* For wrist pieces, I like elastic cord, especially Stretch Magic, which is sturdy, waterproof, comes in several thicknesses, and holds a knot well.

* In a pinch, dental floss, fishing line, yarn, or even raffia or a long blade of grass will do the trick.

* Sturdier beads can handle wire or a fine chain, but the older or more fragile your beads are, the softer and thicker the cord should be in proportion to each bead's hole. This way you'll avoid slippage, clicking, and breaking by padding them from the inside and keeping them from knocking against each other.

* Another way to prevent the beads from hitting and chipping is to tie small overhand knots between them (see page 12).

* I tend to avoid clasps because I like the idea of an unbroken chain—a continuous circle—but if you would prefer to add one, flexible wire is a good bet. Many jewelers recommend soft flex wire. I'm no jeweler, and I don't include projects with clasps in this book, but if you're feeling ambitious, there are many good sources of information from neighborhood craft classes to the Internet. I've found that some of the distributors of jewelry supplies that I've listed in the Resources section (page 125) offer very good explanations.

Finer thread, such as silk beading thread (bottom) is best for light beads, while heavier beads will work better on cord (top).

about knots ...

You will use different types of knots depending on what they're needed for—for example, holding a bead in place or creating space between beads—and also on your personal preference. I've provided instructions on the knots I used for the pieces featured in this book. However, YouTube is also a great resource for finding the right knot for a specific project and it gives you the ability to rewind and practice—and practice again—which is great for those who struggle with knots (like me!). See the Resources section (page 125) for further details.

OVERHAND KNOT

An overhand knot is useful if you want to add a space or cushioning between each bead or extra protection against losing beads if your string breaks. It is simple—the knot you make before tying a bow.

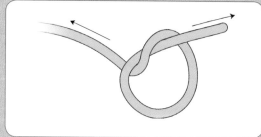

1 Take the left thread over then under the right thread.

2 Pull both ends to secure.

SQUARE KNOT

When it comes to knots, a square knot or reef knot—right over left, and left over right—is a mindful beader's friend and the one I use most of the time when I've finished a project and it comes time to tie it off. It is the best solution for connecting two ends of a string in most instances and can easily be hidden inside a larger bead and secured with a drop of glue or covered with a crimp bead (see page 17).

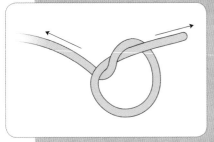 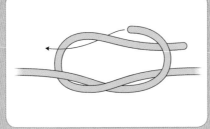 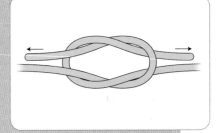

1 Tie an overhand knot, left thread over right thread and under.

2 Take the new right thread over the left thread and under.

3 Pull both ends to secure.

A SURGEON'S KNOT

A surgeon's knot is popular with jewelers for connecting two ends of string. It is so dependable it is what doctors use when suturing incisions.

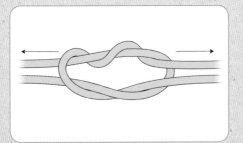

Start by tying a square or reef knot but pass left over right twice and then pull both strings tight.

LARK'S HEAD KNOT

For beads at the center of a necklace, a lark's head knot is often the best solution. I like this knot for many reasons, but especially because it allows you to see the balance of your composition as you work because the thread splits off from the center and you can string in two directions simultaneously.

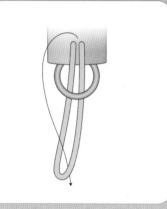

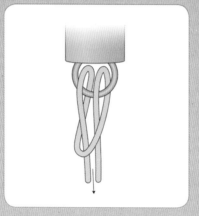

1 Hold both ends of your string together and feed them through the hole or setting.

2 Bring both ends through the loop that the string has formed on the other side of the bead.

3 Pull the ends tight to secure the knot.

some helpful items ...

There's an entire universe of beading gadgetry out there but, fundamentally, all you need is beads and something to string them on. Still, the following may be useful:

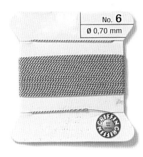

Silk beading string can be bought with a needle woven into the string.

* **Needles** sized for your string and your beads. I prefer very flexible needles with eyes that "grab" the thread, making it easier to work the string through even the tightest bead openings. The large eyes also make them easier to thread. Most craft stores sell silk beading string with the needle woven into the string—these are wonderfully useful because your needle can't come unthreaded while you're working.

* **A piece of cellophane tape** to wrap tightly around the end of your string works well, especially in place of a needle with larger beads, or with thread that is prone to fraying.

* **Glue for securing knots.** A quick-drying epoxy is recommended, but a drop of nail polish will work. It's best to use something waterproof.

* **Small scissors or wire cutters.** Nail clippers are handy for getting close cuts in some situations, especially when working with strong nylon cord or fine wire.

* **Something to hold the end of the string** so that you do not have to tie (and untie) knots. Jewelry supply stores sell all sorts of devices for this, but a large paperclip or a bent metal spring will work, as will tying the end of the string to a spool or simply taping the end to the table.

* It is good to have **something to keep your beads in**. I use a fishing-tackle box because I like the variety of compartment sizes and the way it stows easily when I'm finished, but jars, glasses, plastic bags, or specialty caddies from craft stores are fine as well.

* If you're stringing especially tiny beads, **a magnifying glass**—ideally the kind with a stand and a clip—can be quite useful.

and of course, beads!

My first choice is always my old jewelry box. Second is shopping at independently owned and thoughtfully curated stores, such as Beads of Paradise in New York City (for more stores, see Resources on page 125). Not only will you find the materials you need (and some you did not know you needed but desperately want!), but you'll also be sure to leave with lots of valuable information. I'm also fond of the giant shopping mall that is the Internet, and there are plenty of other options from big-box craft stores to eBay to thrift shops. In the following chapters, and in the Resources section, I'll offer specific suggestions for ways to find beads as well as a few techniques for making your own special ones.

Beads come in so many materials, forms, and sizes, and discovering them is a huge part of the delight of mindful beading. Some types I refer to often in this book:

Seed beads

* **Seed or filler beads**—these are tiny plastic beads shaped like balls or tubes. They're used in various ways from Africa to Slovakia to the Navajo Nation and are available at most craft stores.

* **Focal beads**—these are the large beads at the center of a necklace or bracelet. In malas (Hindu, Buddhist, Jain prayer beads) they are called guru beads, and in Christian rosaries and Islamic misbahah they are the centerpiece and pendant.

* **Pearls**—I prefer Baroque and freshwater pearls because I like the irregular shapes and they tend to be less expensive but there are myriad varieties vastly ranging in price.

Crimp beads

* **Crimp beads** can be bought at most jewelry suppliers. They are small tubes or globes made from an assortment of metals that are useful for hiding knots or joins in a thread or chain. They can be squeezed with pliers to secure joins or even to hide clumsy knots.
* From there, it's limitless—if you can get it onto a string, it's a bead! If you do so with intent or give the process significance, it's mindful.

working mindfully ...

If we're going to be mindful about the process, how we work with our beads matters.

* "A clean, well-lighted place," as Ernest Hemingway famously put it, is key both for our state of mind and the care of our beading supplies.
* Find somewhere quiet and comfortable where you can focus on the action and the intent with which you string the beads. A bright light helps. Discourage cats, if you have any, from jumping on the table. I like to spread a plain white towel out on the surface where I work, because not only does it make it easier to see my supplies but it also prevents the beads from rolling away quite as speedily.

Even if you do not have a special place or dedicated workspace, one of the lovely things about stringing beads is that the process inherently creates an environment of mindfulness. Think about it. The nature of stringing beads is to be calm, still, and focused—like meditation. If your thoughts are scattered your beads will be as well.

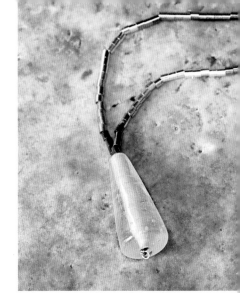

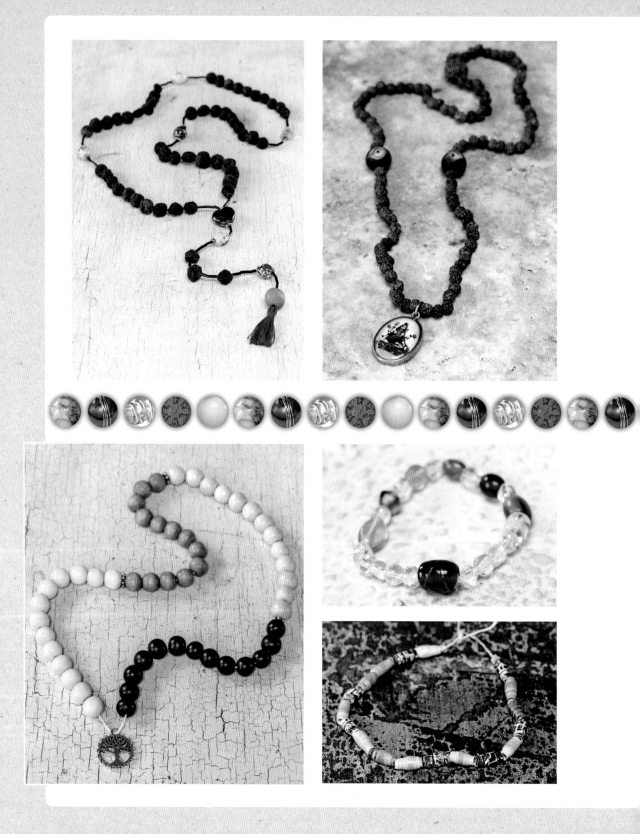

the beads

exploring their meanings
and creating my own

memory strands TIMES & PLACES

As the poet e e cummings famously wrote: "Children are apt to forget to remember." And it is not just children—we all get so involved in the busy-ness of our lives that we lose connection to our best, our most meaningful, and our most joyful memories. Memory strands are a wonderful way to keep those people and occasions we treasure with us always. Think of them as a scrapbook that you get to wear.

The memory strands project completely depends on you and what you want to commemorate—a holiday, place, or time. What do you want to remember? Memory strands are lovely gifts for weddings or graduations or to wear when feeling wistful for a special occasion, a child who has gone off to college, or a very happy-for-no-particular reason time. I've been to memorial services and ordinations where strings of beads were given to the guests and participants, and it was an eloquent way to honor the person being celebrated and carry the reverence of the event into everyday life.

Cape Cod, Massachusetts, is where my family goes on vacation every summer.

creation: MY MEMORY BEADS

My family goes to the seashore in Cape Cod, Massachusetts every summer, and has for decades, so for me, it is a time and season layered with all sorts of wonderful recollections. I decided to bring those to my memory strands. These are the components I chose:

* **Powder-glass beads in sky blue and sea green** from Bali and Ghana. I could not find anything locally sourced that served my purposes quite as well as these, because the colors resonated for me and they reminded me of gathering sea glass.

* **Shells.** Traditional seashells turned into beads are quite easy to acquire—you can gather them and pierce them yourself or buy them. I chose polished shells because they are less fragile and more comfortable to wear on my wrist.

* **Lava beads.** These are available in most craft stores. I added them because they look like the white sand on the beach on a sunny day.

POWDER-GLASS BEADS

"My memory beads evoke the seashore."

LAVA BEADS

SHELLS

MEMORY STRAND POSSIBILITIES

The beads I chose for my bracelet hold my memories. How will you represent your special times and the people you shared them with? Here are some suggestions:

* the ribbon from a baby's dress
* a ring too small or fragile to wear on your hand that looks lovely as a charm
* a single earring from a pair you loved until you lost one
* buttons or zipper pulls from a wedding dress
* a small coin or pebbles picked up on a special vacation (either wrap with wire or drill a small hole)
* birthstones of the people who are part of a wonderful memory

* bobbins to remember sewing with your grandmother
* tiny toys (or parts of toys, such as a train's wheel or a doll's shoe)
* Scouting or military medals
* bubblegum-machine charms
* dice or game pieces from a family favorite, dominoes, or mahjong tiles
* initials or names spelled out in Scrabble tiles or typewriter keys
* keys or pieces of hardware (such as a washer or a tiny hinge) from a childhood home
* a small watch or the gears from a broken timepiece belonging to someone you cherish
* beads with images of animals or flowers to remind you of a favorite pet or garden or season
* simple stones or beads in colors that evoke a happy memory
* acorns, sticks, or feathers from a hike or woodland trail
* guitar picks or clarinet reeds
* a child's drawing or love note photocopied and shrunk way, way down to put into a locket or a tiny frame

Use your imagination! There are as many possibilities as there are people and places you love.

consideration: MEDITATING ON MEMORY

A meditation on memory strands really depends on what or whom you choose to honor. If you used beads to symbolize someone you love, you might recall the words of that person's favorite song or poem—in the case of children, maybe the lullaby you sang to them when they were babies—and then think about how you can help and guide whoever is in your thoughts, hold that person in your heart, or honor the faith he or she had in you. If it is a special time or place, sit for a minute and return to the sensation of that fragrance of a campfire, thrill of seeing the Pacific Ocean for the first time, or the house that will always define home for you. Draw on this state of being when you're going through challenges.

As you meditate on memory, consider reading the verses from Ecclesiastes 3:1-8:

> To every thing there is a season, and a time to every
> purpose under the heaven:
> A time to be born, and a time to die; a time to plant,
> and a time to pluck up that which is planted;
> A time to kill, and a time to heal; a time to break down,
> and a time to build up;
> A time to weep, and a time to laugh; a time to mourn,
> and a time to dance;
> A time to cast away stones, and a time to gather stones together;
> A time to embrace, and a time to refrain from embracing;
> A time to get, and a time to lose; a time to keep, and
> a time to cast away;
> A time to rend, and a time to sew; a time to keep silence,
> and a time to speak;
> A time to love, and a time to hate; a time of war,
> and a time of peace.

Whatever it is that may hold meaning, memory strands are a way to make manifest the words of twentieth-century American poet Theodore Roethke (1908–1963): "What falls away is always. And is near."

heavenly bodies

ASTRONOMY & ASTROLOGY

This cosmic mala is one of my favorites because it is suitable for a scientist, poet, or astrologer. Everyone is inspired by looking at the sky, stars, and planets. Whether you gaze up in order to contemplate astronomical mysteries, such as black holes, determine the earth's position in relation to the sun so as to find the precise times of day and night for prayer, or to help a child with an educational crafts project, this bracelet has a connection to most everyone.

creation: MY HEAVENLY BODY BEADS

The idea is simple—the beads represent heavenly bodies. You can be as precise or impressionistic as you like. For mine, I decided to work out from the sun to the mystery planet that astronomers say lurks beyond Pluto.

Scientists take note—these beads are not to scale! I've approximated, based on beads I found pleasing, the bracelet's weight, and what I had at hand. I chose a large amber bead to stand for the sun and went from there, choosing beads to represent:

* **terrestrial planets**—Mercury, Venus, Earth, and Mars
* **gas giants**—Jupiter and Saturn
* **ice planets**—Uranus and Neptune
* **Pluto** (although some astronomers no longer include this in our solar system)
* and a bead to symbolize **the mysteries beyond** …

I also put in some of the major moons using small silvery gray glass beads. I used gold wire for Saturn's rings and to add a little glimmer. I like the idea of rings moving around on the bracelet, but you could affix them to the planet with a drop of glue.

I'm pleased with how the bracelet turned out and it has led to more than one conversation. This configuration of beads was one that appealed to me, but with a bit

MERCURY

VENUS

THE SUN

THE MOON

EARTH

MARS

MYSTERY PLANET

"All the planets are included on my cosmic mala."

PLUTO

NEPTUNE

JUPITER

SATURN

URANUS

of research you'll find there are many more associations and gems for every heavenly body—from moons to asteroids to planets that no longer exist.

PLANETARY ASSOCIATIONS

If you have the time to research and shop, you could find beads that approximate scale more closely (although there's too much range to be exact), and ones made from substances as close to the planets they stand for as we can find here on Earth. (This could be a great project for a science fair.) For example:

* Mercury's core is thought to have a higher concentration of iron than any of the other planets in our solar system, so including an iron pyrite bead would be a good choice.

* Space exploration has determined that Venus has been shaped by volcanic activity, so lava beads might be a nice option.

* Since about 71% of the Earth's surface is water, you could use aquamarine to evoke that; or you could use a clay bead that is created from earth.

* The core of Mars is made up of metallic iron and nickel and its red color comes from oxidation of iron on its surface, so perhaps choose beads with red iron pyrite inclusions.

* Jupiter's core is obscured by gas, so a smoky quartz bead might be a good representation. Saturn, too, is primarily gas.

* Uranus and Neptune are known as "ice giants," so think about crystalline stones for them.

* Pluto is a rockier planet than its "neighbors," so select a stone that evokes that.

Clockwise from top: pyrite, aquamarine, and smoky quartz.

ASTROLOGICAL ASSOCIATIONS

The more astrologically inclined might like to acknowledge their birth sign by choosing the associated stone, which again varies depending on the source, so pick the ones that mean the most to you!

♈	ARIES	jasper, bloodstone
♉	TAURUS	sapphire, amber, coral
♊	GEMINI	aquamarine, agate
♋	CANCER	moonstone, pearls, emerald
♌	LEO	tourmaline, onyx
♍	VIRGO	jade, carnelian, azurite, zircon
♎	LIBRA	opal, chrysolite
♏	SCORPIO	beryl, topaz, obsidian
♐	SAGITTARIUS	turquoise, citrine
♑	CAPRICORN	diamond, ruby
♒	AQUARIUS	azurite, malachite, garnet
♓	PISCES	aquamarine, amethyst

consideration: CONTEMPLATING OUR PLACE IN THE UNIVERSE

Wear your beads on a night walk, and spend some time considering the infinity of the universe and our small place in it. It will put your troubles in perspective and help you appreciate the mystery and magic of our solar system.

Johannes Kepler (1571–1630) was a German astronomer and mathematician who developed the three laws of planetary motion and was an early proponent of the ideas of Nicolaus Copernicus (1473–1543), who determined that the sun not the earth is the center of our universe. I love how Kepler's "Astronomer's Prayer" contrasts human finiteness with the infinity of space and the Divine. Consider reciting it during your moonlight walks as you hold your beads and contemplate the vastness of space.

An Astronomer's Prayer

I thank You, my Creator,
that You have given me joys
in Your creation and ecstasy over the work
of Your hands.
I have known the glory of Your works
as far as my finite spirit was able to comprehend
Your infinity.
If I have said anything wholly unworthy of You,
or have aspired after my own glory,
graciously forgive me.

Otherwise, you could reread one of my favorite poems by nineteenth-century American poet Walt Whitman (1819–1892):

When I Heard the Learned Astronomer

When I heard the learn'd astronomer;
When the proofs, the figures,
were ranged in columns before me;
When I was shown the charts and the diagrams,
to add, divide, and measure them;
When I, sitting, heard the astronomer,
where he lectured with much applause
in the lecture-room,
How soon, unaccountable, I became tired and sick;
Till rising and gliding out, I wander'd off by myself,
In the mystical moist night-air,
and from time to time,
Look'd up in perfect silence at the stars.

blessed beads MAGIC & ALCHEMY

There are many definitions of magic and alchemy, but for our purposes let's say they both mean using symbols, rituals, and actions directed toward internal transformation. These Blessed Beads are among my favorites to wear, because not only do they make me feel grounded when I'm anxious, but I'm also pleased with how the design turned out.

I love that there was so much symbolism involved in making them—every element means something, starting with the smaller gold, silver, copper, and iron-colored beads. *The Mirror of Alchimy*, published in 1597 and ascribed to English philosopher and friar Roger Bacon (1214–1292), speaks "of the nature of" these metals, and the author adds: "That which has been spoken, every Alchemist must diligently observe." What's so interesting to me about magical and alchemical thinking is that it all comes back to balance—dark and light, above and below, yin and yang, clean and unclean, and perfect and imperfect.

A modern interpretation of the magical and meaningful properties of each metal's associations looks like this:

* **Gold** like the sun, evokes power, protection, energy, strength, and the perfection of matter because it never tarnishes.
* **Silver** reflects the moon, conjuring insight, creativity, pure thought, emotional balance, and transformation.
* **Copper** the metal of Venus, bringing love, peace, luck, health, and connection.
* **Iron** balanced by Mars, in both destruction and construction as it repels negativity, providing grounding and magnetism.

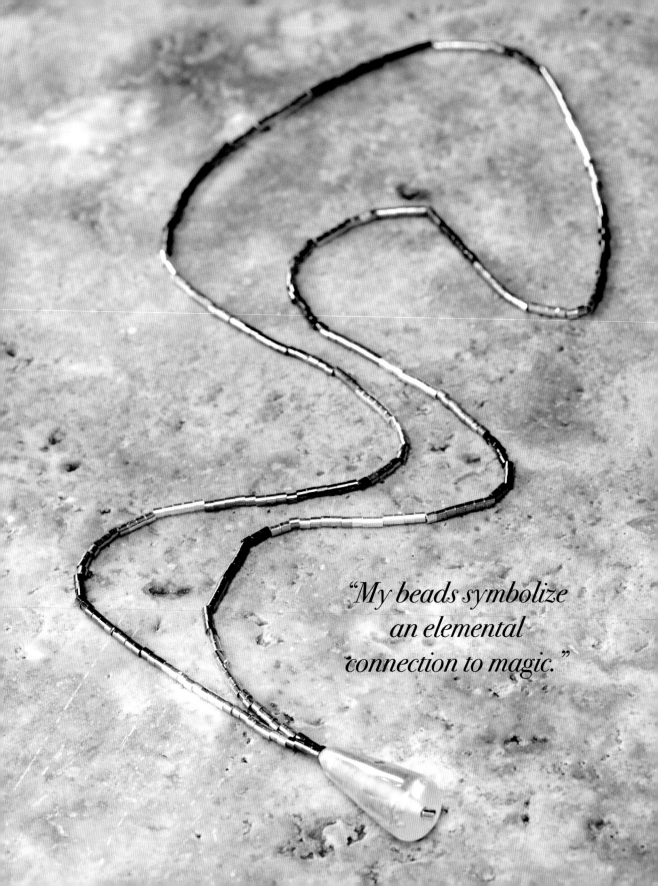

*"My beads symbolize
an elemental
connection to magic."*

creation: MY BLESSED BEADS

This elemental connection to magic is why I chose the sequence of gold, silver, copper, and iron bugle beads—6.5 mm and actually metallic-lined glass. I also like the fluidity of the smaller beads, how even though they are metallic, when I strung them together they took on a liquidity. For me, that suggests alchemy because what appears to be metal also seems to be its opposite.

I strung each type of metal in increments of eight—so eight gold beads, eight silver beads, and so on—to represent the eight pagan Sabbaths.

I liked the idea of marking times that are seen as powerful—often because of the Earth's relationship to the Sun—and of incorporating a whole year of important days into one necklace. It made me think of continuity and how all endings signal beginnings, just as all beginnings must involve ends.

Eight is also sacred in other paradigms. There are eight trigrams, or *pa kua*, in Taoist cosmology, representing the fundamental principles of reality—heaven, wind, mountain, water, earth, thunder, fire, and lake. If you turn an eight on its side (∞) it signifies infinity.

The focal bead I chose struck me as magical in two ways—as a cone and as a pendulum (see practices on page 34). It is made of cloudy glass, which spoke to me of mystery and enchantment. When you string your Blessed Beads, find a focal bead that holds a special meaning for you. Maybe it will be a cone like mine, or perhaps the initial letter of someone's name, an image from nature or sacred geometry, or perhaps a religious symbol, such as a cross, a Sanskrit om, a star of David, or a hand of Fatima.

The pendant at the end of my chain could be seen as a cone of power. There's a belief that energy moves in a conical pattern, gathering at the circular base and rising as it is directed to a precise point. Many see it as the reason for the form of what we regard as traditional witches' hats. This cone of power is often envisioned as light, which this bead seemed to fit.

THE EIGHT PAGAN SABBATHS

Yule or Winter Solstice	December 21	New beginnings
Imbolc	February 1	The hope for spring and dedicating the year
Ostara or Vernal Equinox	March 21	The beginning of spring
Beltane	May 1	First day of summer, fecundity, and joy
Litha or Midsummer Solstice	June 21	The day the sun shines its longest
Lammas	August 1	To mark the first harvest
Mabon or Autumnal Equinox	September 21	Sharing blessings and thanksgiving
Samhain	October 31	Beginning of winter and a time to reflect on people and things that have passed on

(Dates are for the northern hemisphere, and may be adjusted according to season in the south.)

consideration: HARNESSING THE POWER OF YOUR BEADS

There are several ways in which you can work with your Blessed Beads based on the concept of the cone of power, if you have chosen a cone as your focal bead. Try this practice:

1　Hang your Blessed Beads in a window and let the sun or moon spark through them. Sit quietly and appreciate the quiet miracle in the movement of light—the complexity of something we so often take for granted.
2　Focus on the wide end of the cone and allow yourself to be grounded with it as you take time for your energy to gather and develop into strength.
3　In your mind's eye, picture energy traveling from that foundation and concentrating into the point of the cone.
4　When you reach the narrow-most point of the cone, direct that intensified energy toward an issue you face. It might be a specific obstacle, such as a relationship or career challenge, or it might be a personal goal, such as procrastinating less or finding your way toward loving and allowing yourself to be loved.

Another way to look at the focal bead is as a pendulum, which many use as a divination tool. Try it and see if it resonates for you.

1　Clear your mind. Hold your Blessed Beads at the top and let the pendulum swing in space and then settle.
2　Take a deep breath and ask a meaningful question. Speak your question aloud, then pause and focus on the pendulum.
3　It is said that a pendulum will respond positively by moving clockwise and answer "no" by moving counterclockwise. Whether this system appeals to you or not, the process of concentrating on the question as you focus on the pendulum will guide you toward your answer.

Whatever method you choose for working with a challenge or question is sure to have benefits irrespective of the focal bead you have selected—the intent is the important thing, and the choice to focus on the question and seek the answer. You can keep it simple—use your Blessed Beads for meditation by holding them up and allowing the heavy bead to swing, or by hanging them in a window, as described. Focus on them and nothing else. Breath slowly, synchronizing your inhalation and exhalation with the motion of the focal bead as you gradually let go of other distractions, allowing the answer you seek to come to you.

No matter how you may choose to practice with these beads, once you finish the meditation, recite an invocation or prayer to affirm the process. Perhaps you will want to use this interpretation of a blessing, which draws on the time marked by the Sabbaths and the gathered energy of the cone:

"The sun brings the beginning
The moon contains darkness
As above, so below
For there is no greater magic in all the world ..."

Wear your beads knowing that they'll help you live in a place of balance and equilibrium, existing between the earth and the sky—*as above, so below*—guiding you toward your destiny, whatever it may be.

moon and stars TIBET

If you were hoping to make a more traditional mala, this is the project for you! I based these mindful beads on Tibetan Buddhist malas I have seen and admired. Varieties are used throughout Japan, China, Korea, and Sri Lanka as well. They are sometimes called Buddhist rosaries. The Sanskrit word *mala* means "wreath garland"—like a garland of flowers. The word "bead" is etymologically linked to "Buddha." Both those words are rooted in the Sanskrit *budh*, which means "to awaken." This seems like the perfect way to set out to make a string of mindful beads!

creation: MY MOON-AND-STARS MALA

I opted for Tibetan moon-and-star beads because I like their name and because they are a classic choice. Although often called bodhi seeds, the beads are actually rattan plant seeds—hard, ivory-colored (gradually turning a deep golden brown after long use), with holes (symbolizing moons) and dots (symbolizing stars) covering the surface. You can find them online and at many bead suppliers who specialize in Asian beads.

Moon-and-star beads aren't your only possibility. To make a Tibetan-style mala you can also use lotus seeds, yak bone, turquoise, amber, crystal, black lacquer, or sandalwood. I've even read about malas made of nothing but diamonds!

A traditional Tibetan mala has 108 beads. 108 is an auspicious number throughout the East and worldwide, which has many meanings attributed to it (some are listed on page 38). You can also make a mala with 54 or 27 beads, numbers that can be divided into 108—54 for a shorter necklace, 27 for a wrist mala.

I spaced my moon-and-star beads with small glass beads that struck me as both lunar and star-like, and made the neckpiece a little shorter. I also used brown beads sold as bodhi seeds (most likely dried and polished lotus seeds) to make the piece a little less heavy.

"I based my Moon-and-Stars mala on traditional Tibetan meditation beads."

THE AUSPICIOUS NUMBER 108

* 108 is said to be the number representing spiritual completion or awakening.
* The number of desires Buddhists believe we cling to, or emotions or impurities of mind that become obstacles to our awakening.
* One of the circles of stones within Stonehenge is 108 feet in diameter.
* Some religions believe there are 108 paths to God and 108 ways to pray.
* The words of the Buddha—in Tibetan the *Kangyur*—are divided into 108 volumes.
* The Buddhist scriptures tell us that the Bodhisattva Mahamati asked the Buddha 108 questions.

Most malas culminate in a focal bead, and mine is a beautiful Chinese wooden carving of the Buddha's face—a bead I found while shopping with a friend on a special outing, so I guess that makes this a memory strand as well! (See page 20.) The hole at the bottom of the carving is quite large, so I added a tassel to secure it in place.

This larger bead in a mala is often referred to as the "guru bead" because it reminds us of our guru or spiritual teacher—whoever that may be within whatever tradition we practice. Practically speaking, the guru bead provides a beginning and ending point if we want to use the mala to keep track as we count 108 prayers, breaths, bows, or recitations of the Buddha's or God's name. Halfway up the strands on either side of the guru bead, I added a single gold- and silver-painted rudraksha bead, again to evoke the moon and the stars.

consideration: MEDITATING WITH YOUR MALA

Tibetan Buddhists recite many different mantras as part of their meditation practices. The most often heard is *Om mani padme hum*, the Tibetan chant of love and compassion. Loosely translated from the Sanskrit it means "The jewel within the lotus" or "Praise to the jewel in the lotus." There are myriad interpretations of this very important mantra, of which His Holiness the Fourteenth Dalai Lama has said:

"The six syllables [...] mean that in dependence on the practice which is in indivisible union of method and wisdom, you can transform your impure body, speech, and mind into the pure body, speech, and mind of a Buddha."

Chanting mantras uses sound to move our beings from the physical to the spiritual as the sacred words resonate through our bodies. You might want to try reciting *Om mani padme hum* or another text that is meaningful for you, and counting the recitations with your mala. Whether you're a novice meditator or have been practicing for a while, you can use your mala as you count your breath. Try this:

1. Sit in a comfortable position and hold your mala in your dominant hand—your right if you're right-handed and your left if you're left-handed.
2. Grasp the guru or largest bead between two fingers and concentrate on your intention. It can be as simple as a desire to stay focused and undistracted. Now, let go of that thought. Breathe in … and breathe out.
3. Slide your fingers to the next bead and again breathe in and then out. Look at your thoughts as they arise—do not judge them, just look at them—and then nudge them out of your consciousness like clouds out of a blue sky.
4. Move to the next bead and then the next, until you return to the main bead.
5. Sit for a moment to connect with the experience. Thank yourself for taking the time to be mindful and meditate, and thank the universe for giving you the opportunity to be able to do so.

When you're finished with your mala, put it in a safe place—perhaps a little silk jewelry bag or a designated box. Tibetan Buddhists believe that, like sacred texts, malas represent the Buddha and so we should treat them with reverence.

veneration CHRISTIANITY

Many people in the West think of rosaries when considering beads associated with prayer and spirituality, and perhaps even recall the Prioress in Geoffrey Chaucer's classic, *The Canterbury Tales*:

> "Of small coral about her arm she bare
> A pair of beades, gauded all with green;
> And thereon hung a brooch of gold full sheen,
> On which was first written a crowned A,
> And after, Amor vincit omnia ..."

***Amor vincit omnia*—"Love conquers all things." In the Prioress's tale, she speaks of the Virgin Mary to whom rosaries are traditionally dedicated and prayers are recited. Mary is the historical mother of Jesus and an emblem of purity.**

Praying with the rosary became widespread in medieval European monasteries. Using beads or small stones to count prayers is likely as old as prayer itself. Legend has it that the Virgin Mary first revealed the rosary to Saint Dominic in a vision. Saint Dominic (1170–1221) was the founder of the Catholic Dominican Order and the patron saint of astronomy. However, it is most often agreed that thirteenth-century writer and theologian Thomas of Cantimpré was the first to call the chain of prayer a "rosary," since the faithful used strung rose petals and beads made of crushed rose petals to count prayers. It's said that "rosary" came from the Latin *rosarium*, meaning a "rose garden" or "garland of roses."

The rose has long been associated with the Virgin Mary, who is sometimes referred to as "the mystical rose" or "the rose without thorns." In Catholicism, the rose represents perfection, and each color variation of the flower has a special significance, the rosary becoming a garden for prayer. For example, red for self-sacrifice and martyrdom and white for purity.

Traditionally, a rosary is made of 59 beads and a crucifix:

* Fifty beads are divided into five sets of ten. Each set (or decade, as it is called) is linked to what are known as the mysteries, events from the lives of Jesus and Mary, to be contemplated while reciting the "Hail Mary" prayer, once for each bead. These mysteries are categorized as Joyful, Sorrowful, Glorious, and Luminous. The Luminous mysteries include the baptism of Jesus, the miracles he performed at the wedding at Cana, Jesus speaking of the return of the Kingdom of God, the Transfiguration of Jesus when he becomes the illumination of God, and the Eucharist or the transformation of wine and bread into the body of God.

Rosaries are used for prayer and contemplation.

* Five larger beads divide the decades. The Lord's Prayer and the "Glory Be" prayer are said here.
* One of these larger beads is the focal bead, often a pendant, which leads to a single strand. This bead is often used to signal another recitation of The Lord's Prayer.
* The single strand has four more beads, three to indicate faith, hope, and charity and the reciting of three more "Hail Mary" prayers, and one larger one for a "Glory Be" or the Apostles' Creed.
* The rosary begins and culminates in a cross where one might make a request for guidance and mercy, such as reciting this line from Psalm 69: "Oh God, come to my assistance; Oh Lord, make haste to help me."

creation: MY VENERATION ROSARY

Beads can be made from olive pits, coral, pearls, amethyst, sapphire, or bloodstone. Many materials are associated with legends and symbolism. You might want to try topaz, which is sacred to Saint Hildegard von Bingen, the twelfth-century German Benedictine abbess, musician, science writer, and mystic, who prayed that she might persevere in God's service; or Saint Cuthbert's beads—beadlike fossils sometimes known as sea lilies, said to be used by this Celtic monk, hermit, and patron saint of northern England. If you have no beads, tying knots into a strand of yarn or cord can serve the same purpose and create a nice effect.

Rosary beads can still be made from rose petals, which is especially apt considering their name and history. They're easy to create, and fragrant! Find out how to make them on pages 44–45.

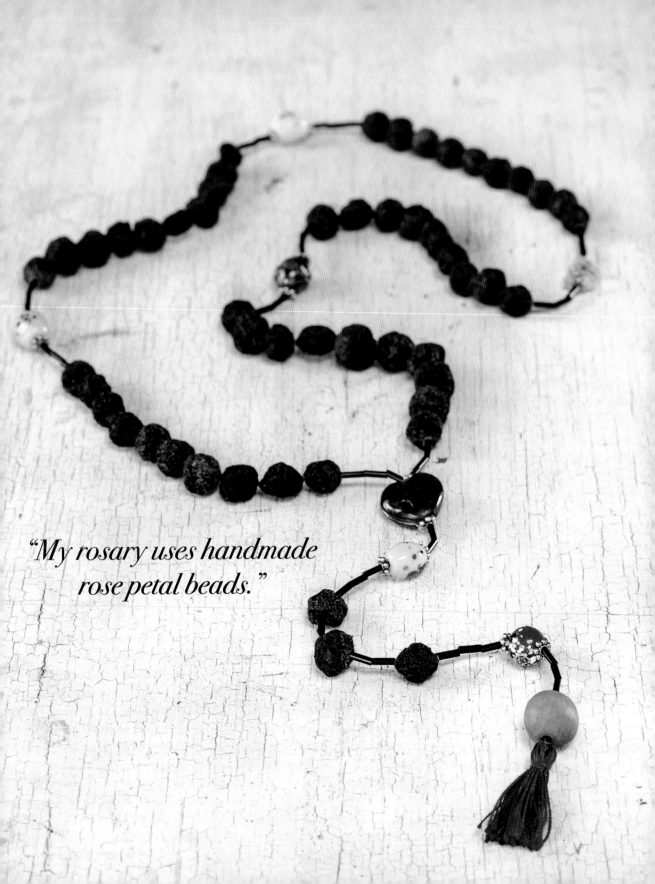

*"My rosary uses handmade
rose petal beads."*

HOW TO MAKE ROSE PETAL BEADS

1 Collect petals from about a dozen roses. Use only the petals and not the other parts of the flower. These do not have to be freshly picked but shouldn't be dried either. You could use a Valentine's Day bouquet as it begins to fade, wedding flowers, a centerpiece, or roses from your garden.

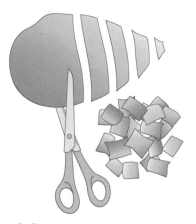

2 Chop the petals on a cutting board, snip them with scissors, or pulse briefly in a blender, if you have one.

3 Put into a pot with barely enough water to cover. Distilled water is believed to result in a purer scent. Cast-iron pots will give the beads a darker color.

4 Cook the rose petals until they are mushy. Stir often and let them come close to a boil but don't actually boil them.

5 When the petals are translucent, take the pan off the heat and let the mixture cool thoroughly.

6 Use a blender (hand-held is fine), food processor, or mortar and pestle to pulverize your petals until they are as smooth as you can make them. Add a little liquid if you need to. They should end up being the consistency of very smooth mashed potatoes.

7 Put the rose "dough" back into the pot and simmer until any liquid has evaporated. Aim for a texture and consistency like Play-Doh or clay. Experiment by adding a couple of drops of rose oil or some flakes of gold leaf.

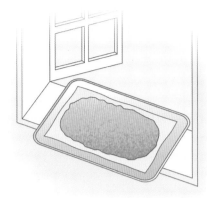

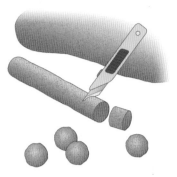

8 Spread the rose dough on a cookie sheet covered with waxed paper and let it sit in a warm dry place (a sunny window or an oven with a pilot light) for 24 hours.

9 Once the dough is malleable, cut and roll it into the size and shape you'd like your beads to be.

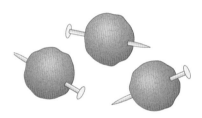

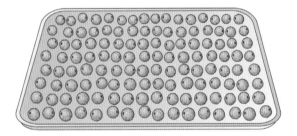

10 Pierce the beads with small nails, opened paper clips, or straight pins, depending on how big you'd like the holes to be, and leave these in place in the beads for about 24 hours. Gently rotate your beads occasionally so they don't stick to the metal. (Be sure to use something metal to create the holes, because the dough will stick to toothpicks.)

11 Remove the beads from whatever you used to pierce them and spread them on a cookie sheet or platter and leave in a cool dry place for about a week. Be patient with this—it's a mindfulness practice in itself. My first few attempts failed because the weather was humid and the beads weren't thoroughly dried.

12 After you've strung your beads, take care of them. They're fragile so don't get them wet. Also, allow them a little air—if you store them in plastic they can get moldy.

HANDMADE
ROSE BEADS

GLASS FLOWER BEAD

METAL
WASHER BEAD

HEART-SHAPED
FOCAL BEAD

WOODEN BEAD

TASSEL

MAKING MY ROSARY

1   I chose a twisted silk thread and
    attached a wooden bead (to
    represent humility) to a tassel, in lieu
    of a traditional crucifix.

2   I beaded up from the tassel, through
    the heart-shaped focal bead (chosen
    to represent love), and continued
    along in increments of 10 to make the
    main loop.

3   I separated the decades with glass
    beads that looked flowery to expand
    upon the rose and flower theme,
    and because they gave the piece
    some light.

4   I used metal beads as washers around
    the floral beads to separate them
    from the small black cylindrical filler
    beads that I strung before and after
    the rose beads.

5   I went back through the focal bead,
    tied off the end, and tucked it in there
    since it's a larger bead.

6   The rose beads were a bit tough to
    string because they had different-sized
    holes—they're handmade so don't
    dry evenly—and the holes were
    sometimes hard to find.

consideration:
PRAYING WITH YOUR ROSARY

Part of the beauty and mystique of praying with the rosary is the repetition. Repeating the prayers takes you deeper into the language, making you more mindful of each word, until you eventually stop thinking and embody, or perhaps even become, the prayers. If the traditional prayers resonate for you in a profound way, try spending some time using your rosary to keep count so that your mind and heart can focus on the intent and meaning of the words. You don't have to limit yourself to the Lord's Prayer and Hail Mary. There may be other liturgies or prayers, poems, or texts from sacred literature that mean more to you, and if so, choose one of those.

Your prayers can be as elaborate as you like or as simple as saying "*Amor vincit omnia*" or "*Dona nobis pacem*" meaning "Grant us peace" 60 times. Mindfully speaking and concentrating on these words as a prayer, a wish, or a mantra will center and uplift you, no matter your faith or culture.

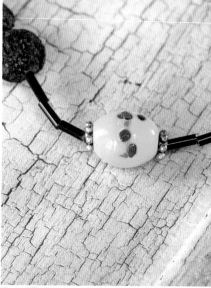

power beads MAASAI

Beads are so very important and varied in African culture that it is said there may well be over 40 words to describe them, kind of like the Eskimos having more than a hundred words for snow. Beads are especially meaningful to the Maasai people, who live in southern Kenya and northern Tanzania along Africa's Great Rift Valley. The Maasai have long been admired for protecting and keeping their culture intact despite outside influences, and one way they have done this is with their intricate, symbolic, and distinctive beaded jewelry. For the Maasai, beadwork is not merely about aesthetics and decoration but is representative of identity and status within the community.

For centuries, beads were made from natural materials, such as shell, wood, seeds, and stone. Later, during the nineteenth century, the Maasai incorporated glass beads as European trade, travel, and settlement developed.

There are myriad examples of beads used in rituals, including weddings. An intriguing one is "the ceremony of the red bead," which British author Sir Alfred Claud Hollis (1874–1961) described in his 1905 book, *The Maasai: Their Language and Folklore*:

The colors of Maasai power beads all have meanings.

"When a Maasai wishes to make a person his brother or sister, he gives that person a red bead, called ol-tureshi. After performing this ceremony, they call one another Patureshi, i.e. "The giver and receiver of a bead," instead of by their proper names."

Maasai power beads convey specific meanings based on their colors. It is not an exact science, of course, but drawing on a variety of sources I have discovered that within Maasai traditions:

* **Red** is for bravery, strength, unity. Said to be the color of the blood of a slaughtered cow, feasted upon when a community gathers.
* **Blue** is for energy and everything potent, mighty, and powerful that comes from the sky—light, heat, rain, wind—and water.
* **Green** is for health, putting down roots, and protection. It is the color of verdant crops and fields.
* **Orange** is for friendship, hospitality, warmth, and generosity. It is the color of animal skins used to decorate homes and cover beds.
* **Yellow** is for sun, fertility, and growth.
* **White** is for purity, health, and peace. The color of the milk of cows, valued and revered because they are the Maasai people's primary food source —a gift from god and a symbol of economic status.
* **Black** is for unity, harmony, the benevolent nature of God, and solidarity to overcome struggles.

creation: MY POWER BEADS

The dignity and courage of the Maasai combined with the bold colors of their beads made me think of empowerment, the idea behind Maasai power beads. There are times when we all feel uncertain, even powerless, and we can use these beads to be mindful of our fears as we work to overcome them. When you create your beads, pick the colors that help you to focus on a specific goal or obstacle. Perhaps you will want to

"These seven bracelets channel the power of the sky and sea."

add a red bead, or several, into a strand that you make as a gift for a friend.

The beads I chose were blue glass for energy and the power of the sky and sea. I interspersed these with beads made from powdered or recycled glass, because for me this implies power as well—reusing the material instead of throwing it away, continuing to give it purpose. They are strung on simple elastic, tied off with a square knot, hidden in a bead.

I made seven bracelets of varying sizes because when worn in a stack they evoke the necklaces worn by Maasai warriors.

consideration: YOUR INNATE POWER

As you string your Power Beads, be mindful of the obstacle you are seeking to overcome. Imbue the process with your intent to be stronger than those things that challenge you.

There is a traditional Maasai song or prayer that requests: *Meishoo iyiook enkai inkishu o-nkera*, which means, "May the Creator bestow cattle and children upon us." Think about this in the context of your own life in whatever way you may interpret personal and spiritual strength (like Maasai do cattle) and the hope for the future that children represent. Wear your beads as a reminder of your innate power—your true self—that you can draw on in all situations, no matter how difficult.

ghost seeds and spirit beads
NATIVE AMERICAN

This is one of the simplest projects in the book, but still one of my favorites. Not only do I love the lore behind ghost seeds and the process of making them, but also the bracelet is light and simple and feels good on my wrist. Native American spiritual beliefs vary depending upon the diverse individual tribes and clans, but they all share a foundation in and reverence for nature, and wearing my spirit seeds helps me to be mindful and connect to that.

Navajo ghost seeds are said to symbolize the link between humankind and the natural world. It is believed that they protect the wearer from evil spirits, ghosts, and nightmares. Traditionally, juniper berries (which are actually seeds but called berries) were collected after they had fallen on the ground and insects had eaten both the fleshy exterior and interior of the seed, leaving behind a hollowed case. The seeds were dried and sometimes held over a fire and smoked to preserve them.

As the beads were strung, a different bead was incorporated to stand out—an "intentional mistake," called a spirit bead. According to Z. Susanne Aikman, who is of Native American descent, a spirit bead is necessary because we are human and inherently imperfect. In *The Art of Native American Beadwork* (11th edition published in 1992), she recommends this practice, suggesting that attempting to achieve perfection could be bad luck.

This one "intentional mistake" reminds me of the Japanese aesthetic concept of *wabi-sabi*, which teaches that beauty is impermanent, imperfect, and incomplete—a form of perfection in itself for Daisetz Teitaro Suzuki. In *Zen and Japanese Culture* (first published in 1938) he suggests that this ultimately illustrates the essence of Zen, or at least how it is often perceived—"the One remaining as one in the Many individually and collectively."

creation: MY GHOST SEED BRACELET

Making this bracelet is quite straightforward—just a matter of stringing seeds and adding a spirit bead. I bought my juniper beads online and chose a turquoise bead for the spirit bead, because the stone is considered sacred in Native American and other cultures.

You might be interested to know that it is not difficult to craft your own juniper seed ghost beads. The process is quite simple and juniper trees grow almost everywhere in the world—throughout the northern hemisphere, from Africa to the Arctic, the Himalayas to Central America. Find out how to make them on pages 54–55.

JUNIPER SEEDS

TURQUOISE BEAD

"The turquoise spirit bead represents an intentional mistake."

HOW TO MAKE JUNIPER SEED GHOST BEADS

1 The first step is to gather the berries—the seed cones of the juniper tree or bush. You can harvest them whenever you find them as long as they are ripe, but late spring through summer tends to be best.

Opt for the ones that are darker blue and have what looks to be a thin coating of white powder on the surface. The green berries can dry too hard and be challenging to work with.

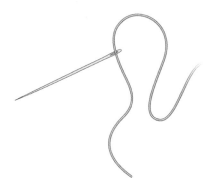

2 String a strong and sharp-pointed needle with monofilament or thread with nylon in it.

3 Take a berry and squeeze it to open the stem part that was connected to the tree—let's call this the top of the berry.

 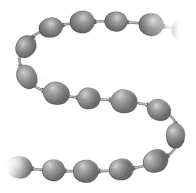

4 Pierce the berry from top to bottom —through the stem—and string it onto your thread. Keep doing this until you run out of thread or berries.

5 If you're going to wear the beads on this thread, ease them close together so your strand won't have gaps. I like to keep my options open, so I left some space between beads so that I can use them for assorted projects, and so that they would dry more evenly.

6 When you've finished stringing the berries, knot the ends of the thread, using a loose knot that can be untied easily, and hang the strand to dry in a well-ventilated spot. They'll dry more quickly in a sunny place, but if you're patient, this doesn't matter—just make sure the drying area is not damp.

7 Leave your ghost seeds there for about three weeks, until they are fully dry. You'll know because they'll be dark brown or black and there will be no "give" when you squeeze them.

consideration: LIVING WITH NATURE

The natural quality of these beads—seeds
and stone—and the many important Native
American teachings about reverence for nature
make me want to practice with these spirit
seeds outdoors or while looking at the
landscape through a window. We all need to
take time to appreciate the greatness of the
natural world—trees and oceans, animals and
mountains, earth and sky—and our small yet
important place within it. As you do so, you
might want to recite this brief prayer from the
Chinook Psalter:

"May all things move and be moved in me,
And know and be known in me
May all creation dance for joy within me."

Maybe this lovely Pueblo blessing will speak to you:

"Hold on to what is good even if it is a handful of earth.
Hold on to what you believe even if it is a tree
which stands by itself.
Hold on to what you must do even if it is a long way from here.
Hold on to life even when it is easier letting go.
Hold on to my hand even when I have gone away from you."

Or maybe you just want to sit quietly and listen to the wind.

chakra lights YOGA

In Sanskrit, chakra means circle or light, so a continuous string of beads—a bracelet or a necklace—is an especially apt way to reflect this meaning. Some yoga practitioners describe chakras as the astral doors through which our physical self connects with our spiritual self.

In yoga and ayurvedic teachings, the seven chakras are the vortexes in which "subtle" energy resides in our bodies and through which it moves. They connect our physical, emotional, and psychological well-being to the spiritual, and reflect our inner states.

Understanding our chakras and the flow of energy is valuable for all sorts of body work, not just yoga. It is helpful to be aware of them if we're dancing, playing sports, making love, or holding a child. The more conscious we become of chakras, the better we can connect to the ebb and flow between our physical, mental, and spiritual selves.

Each chakra is associated with specific attributes, some of which are listed in the chart overleaf.

CROWN CHAKRA

THIRD EYE CHAKRA

THROAT CHAKRA

HEART CHAKRA

SOLAR PLEXUS CHAKRA

NAVEL CHAKRA

ROOT CHAKRA

CHAKRA	MENTAL	PHYSICAL	SPIRITUAL	ASSOCIATED GEMSTONES	ASSOCIATED COLOR
Crown *Sahaswara*	realizing the interconnection of all things, resilience	out-of-body bliss, ability to be still	divine connection, prayer, reflection, meditation	amethyst, moonstone, sapphire, selenite	violet
Third eye (between the eyebrows) *Ajna*	meditation, choosing wisdom and fulfillment in every part of life	knowing, thinking	insight, imagination, clear vision for the future	lapis lazuli, blue topaz, blue chalcedony	indigo
Throat *Vishuddha*	communication, truthfulness, integrity	sense of hearing, back and spinal strength	expressing one's highest purpose and truth, living a creative life	blue lace agate, aquamarine, turquoise, angelate	blue
Heart *Anahata*	learning to love yourself and others, healing	sense of touch, dancing	love, altruism, peace, purity	malachite, emerald, labradorite, green tourmaline	green
Solar plexus (below the breast bone) *Manipura*	self-confidence, joy, self-esteem	sense of sight, competitive athletics	leadership, valuing solitude	citrine, gold tiger's eye, yellow jasper, golden calcite	yellow
Navel *Svadhisthana*	creativity, following through on goals, knowing yourself, developing healthy boundaries	sense of taste, dancing, swimming, walking	well-being, pleasure, sense of abundance	carnelian, amber, bloodstone	orange
Root (at the base of the spine or tailbone) *Muladhara*	patience, passion, perseverance	sense of smell, physical presence and grounding or steadiness	seeing the magic and beauty all around you.	red jasper, garnet, ruby	red

creation: MY CHAKRA BRACELET

Select a chakra you want to pay special attention to, one that needs tending. Perhaps it is the heart because you want to focus on being more loving and altruistic, or the throat because you want to be more mindful of the things you say. Choose a bead of the appropriate color for each chakra (see chart, opposite) and as you string them (in order of the chakras—see page 57), make the one representing your chosen chakra stand out by choosing a larger or more distinct bead. I set off the indigo bead because I want to use my bracelet to help me focus on devoting more energy and attention to meditation through my third eye. I put clear glass in between my chakra beads, because for me this evokes light and energy.

Each chakra is associated with specific gemstones as well as a color. Some are shown in the chart opposite. I chose glass for my chakra bracelet because a strand of gemstones can get pricey, but they would make for a very fancy necklace, so if you have an unlimited budget, go for it! Or you could use glass for every bead except for the chakra you want to pay special attention to and splurge on that one. You could even represent the shape as well as the material— so perhaps a malachite heart or an eye-shaped piece of lapis lazuli.

"My chakra bracelet helps me focus my energy."

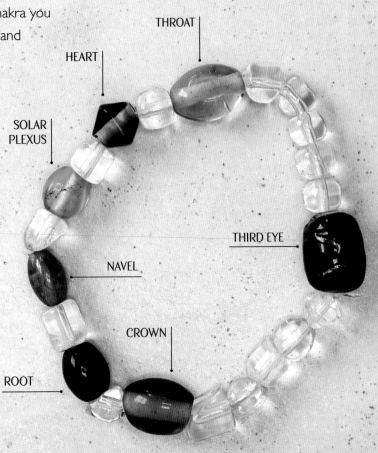

THROAT

HEART

SOLAR PLEXUS

THIRD EYE

NAVEL

ROOT

CROWN

consideration: ALIGNING YOUR CHAKRAS

Healers, yogis, and other spiritual guides perform a practice of chakra alignment wherein they ask their subjects to lay down and then place the associated stones on or near the seven corresponding chakra points. They meditate or use healing touch or chants to work with subtle energy challenges or troubling areas.

You could personalize the practice, using your Chakra Lights bracelet like this:

* Lay down in a comfortable position and place the bracelet at the point in your body that you're concentrating on. Maybe you want to ease a broken heart, or to speak more kindly to those who frustrate you; or maybe you want to foster your creativity or self-confidence.

* Breathe into each chakra—three rounds of seven, so 21 deep slow breaths.

* When you reach the chakra point you're working on, pause, and slowly exhale as you bring your mind to the challenge.

* Perhaps as you finish you'll want to recite these lines written by an anonymous author:

"May we walk with grace
And may the light of the universe
Shine upon our path."

* Then you could read and contemplate this lovely passage written by Sri Anandamayi Ma (1896–1982), one of the great Hindu saints of the twentieth century. Consider each chakra as you sit with her words:

> "Streams of life and of vital fluid course swiftly or slowly through those channels and guide the life-processes and thought-currents of man. Just as you find that earth, water, fire, air, and the space beyond the atmosphere, interpenetrate one another, so also these ... centres lie inside the body apparently one above the other, but functioning in mutual interdependence as one vital chain. A little reflection will convince you that the play of life goes on in the upper centres of your body when your thoughts are pure and full of bliss."

Once you've finished your chakra meditation, put on your bracelet, and wear it as you go about your day, using it as a reminder of how you're energized and clear and how your chakra point has been illuminated.

four elements CELTIC

I imagine the term "mindfulness" had yet to be coined in 1893, when Irish poet W.B. Yeats (1865–1939) wrote of his birthright in "The Celtic Twilight," and yet, he presents the concept perfectly:

> "We gave ourselves up in old times to mythology, and saw the Gods everywhere. We talked to them face to face, and the stories of that communion are so many that I think they outnumber all the like stories of all the rest of Europe ... We can make our minds so like still water that beings gather about us that they may see, it may be, their own images, and so live for a moment with a clearer, perhaps even with a fiercer life because of our quiet."

It is that quiet, that "mind like still water," that allows us to connect to religion, magic, the universe, and ultimately ourselves regardless of our spiritual traditions.

Most spiritual roots tap into the four elements—air, fire, earth, water—and Celtic mysticism is no different. The Celts were a people dwelling primarily in Great Britain and Europe from the Iron Age into the Medieval period. They shared a language, rich cultures, and an approach to things spiritual. Their legends, art, and lore continue to fascinate and inspire us. The early Celtic polytheistic religion associated deities with natural

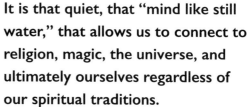

ELEMENT	CELTIC GOD/ GODDESS	DESCRIPTION	CARDINAL POINT	ASSOCIATIONS
Air	Daghdha	The god of magic and wisdom	East	Intellect, mobility
Fire	Ceridwen	The goddess of rebirth	North	Spirituality, transformation
Earth	Dana	The protector, mother of gods	West	Ethereal, purification
Water	Lugh	Storm god, warrior hero	South	Arts, truth

elements and that is where I drew the inspiration for my Four Elements beads. There are countless Celtic gods and goddesses and just as many myths to describe them, but four that I was drawn to were Daghdha, Ceridwen, Dana, and Lugh, because of their association with the four elements (see above).

Another pattern of four featuring the elements in Celtic lore is the quartet of otherworldly cities where the Celtic deities—Tuatha de Danann, or the children of Dana—were said to have mastered their arts and magic: Findias was associated with air, Gorias with fire, Falias with earth, and Murias with water.

creation:
MY FOUR ELEMENTS BRACELETS

I approached these mindful beads with thoughts of Celtic lore and an appreciation for the division yet interconnection of the four elements. Consequently, these are the beads I chose:

* **Amazonite** for the green earth: healing, integrity, and trust
* **Sunstone** for fire: positive thoughts, joy, and balance
* **Moonstone** for air: intuition, and perception
* **Seed pearls** for water: focus

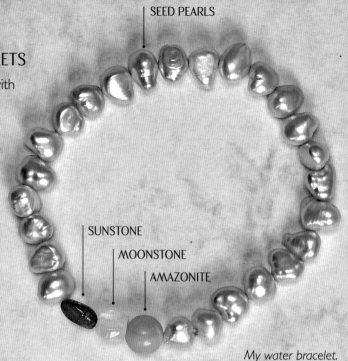

SEED PEARLS

SUNSTONE

MOONSTONE

AMAZONITE

My water bracelet.

I made a string of each of these. On the strings of sunstone, moonstone, and pearls, I included one of each of the other three beads I had chosen, along with the primary beads. The exception was amazonite and this was for practical reasons—the bracelet did not sit well with the smaller beads in it and besides, I like how these "earth" beads ground the other three bracelets.

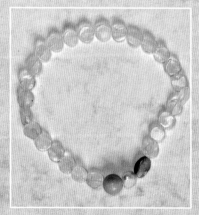

My other element bracelets, left to right: earth, air, and fire.

consideration: THAT WHICH UPLIFTS AND INSPIRES

The mysteries of the Druids and Celtic mythology inspired Irish author AE (George William Russell, 1867–1935), who wrote in his 1918 book, *The Candle of Vision*:

> "... try to become the master of your vision, and seek for and evoke the greatest of earth memories, not those things which only satisfy curiosity, but those which uplift and inspire, and give us a vision of our own greatness; and the noblest of all Earth's memories is the august ritual of the ancient mysteries, where the mortal, amid scenes of unimaginable grandeur, was disrobed of his mortality and made of the company of the gods."

What a remarkable thing to practice! As you wear your Four Elements beads, use them as a reminder to be mindful and visualize connecting to that part of yourself that uplifts and inspires, until you arrive at something greater than yourself.

healing CRYSTALS

Crystals are the stuff of gems—pure stones composed of atoms arranged in a regular geometric pattern. It is not the sparkle that makes crystals, but the form minerals take when they solidify. Their internal structure—the regularly repeating arrangement of atoms—is mirrored by their external structure. It is the same with people—who we are on the inside is reflected on the outside.

Beyond being fascinating and beautiful, crystals are considered energetically powerful in Tibet, Australia, and the Americas, and many people attribute all sorts of healing abilities to them from physical to psychological to spiritual. How crystals work is the subject of considerable debate—minerals certainly interact with light and other kinds

Crystal jewelry can be used for healing.

of radiation just as electricity, magnetism, and radiation all interact with the body, for good and for ill.

I believe neuroscience can offer some insights. Since the neurons in our brains that fire together wire together, it is possible that even simply thinking about healing when we look at, or meditate with, our crystal beads will create a state conducive for that healing to take place. Intention and belief are key elements of the process, as is, perhaps, the placebo effect—the scientific truth that beneficial outcomes can be attributed to brain/mind responses to the context in which healing is delivered rather than to the specific actions of a substance.

If association with a specific crystal (or group of them) can foster a mindset that stimulates healing, our next step is to choose what we'd like to heal. It could be a physical or mental problem, an obstacle, anxiety, or habit.

For example, Philip Permutt in his comprehensive book *The Crystal Healer* recommends:

* jasper and peridot to lift our mood
* amethyst and onyx to ease grief
* citrine and topaz to help us work with indecision

Another way to approach crystals, which I find interesting, is to apply them to one's job or vocation. In her *Essential Guide to Crystals, Minerals, and Stones*, author Margaret Ann Lembo makes connections between professions and crystals, including:

* artist—blue topaz and carnelian
* caregiver—hematite and Isis quartz
* inventor—bloodstone and blue topaz
* parent—black tourmaline and blue lace agate
* spiritual counselor—amethyst and
  clear quartz

From top, left to right: tourmaline, quartz, carnelian, topaz, onyz, amethyst, blue lace agate, citrine, bloodstone, peridot, jasper, and hematite.

"The septarian focal bead brings patience."

creation: MY HEALING CRYSTAL NECKLACE

As with all mindful bead projects, the best choice is the stone that speaks to you. When beginning with crystals, first discover which types direct energy to those things you want to heal or work with. There are tons of resources out there—in bookstores and on the Internet—or go with your gut and intuition. Maybe the color, the shape, a memory or association, or the feeling you get when you hold a stone will guide your choice.

I decided I wanted to direct energy toward something I find tremendously challenging—patience. I am an impatient person (to say the least) so I decided to use crystals to address that issue. I also wanted to challenge the preconceived notion of crystals, emphasizing that they can be about intention and do not have to be pink and sparkly (unless, of course, that's what you're in the mood for). I had no clue which ones were associated with patience, so I again referred to Philip Permutt's book, and was drawn to:

PINK ARAGONITE

RUTILATED QUARTZ

HEMATITE

SEPTARIAN

* **Septarian,** an amazing-looking calcium carbonate or carbonate of iron that has cracks filled with other lighter-colored minerals. It is associated with patience.

* **Rutilated quartz,** also called "angel hair," which pleases me. This is another crystal with an intriguing appearance—black rods shooting through the clear stone. Philip Permutt writes that it is good for mental health, brings balance and calm, and eliminates negativity, which works for me since I see my impatience as a negative habit.

* **Hematite,** which I incorporated for visual (and maybe even psychic) balance. It is not specifically suggested for patience, but I liked the idea of including this because Phillip Permutt believes it brings strength and love, plus it is said to be grounding—all things from which I can benefit.

* Finally, I included **pink aragonite** because it's said to be good for problem-solving, and for combating stress and anger, and because it added some brightness to the project.

Crystals tend to be heavier than most beads, so I decided to make a necklace using a strong silk thread. When I tried to make a bracelet, it felt too clunky and hard to live with. I chose septarian as the focal bead, not only for its association with patience, but because it has such a remarkable appearance and I found a beautiful piece of it that was already drilled and included a wire loop for stringing. To secure the focal bead, I opted for a lark's head knot (see page 14) and from there I strung up both sides.

I balanced this central pendant (focal bead) with two rutilated quartz crystals a little way up either side. Between these and the focal bead I mixed in the hematite, aragonite, and seed filler beads to add a little light as I worked my way along the strands. When the strands met, I tied one to the other with a square knot (see page 13) and hid it in a hematite bead, secured with a drop of glue.

consideration: MEDITATIONS FOR HEALING

To bring myself back to a place of patience and connection, I like to hold my healing crystals and recite this version of a Buddhist chant:

"May suffering ones be suffering free
May the fear-struck fearless be.
May grieving ones progress through grief—
May all be healed and find relief."

Otherwise, you could think about a line from Saint Francis de Sales, who famously said "have patience with everyone, but first of all with yourself."

Perhaps you have another prayer or poem that suits you and brings you to a place that facilitates healing yourself or others. I have a friend who likes to a recite a few lines from the prayer attributed to a different Saint Francis—Saint Francis of Assisi:

"That where there are shadows, I may bring light.
That where there is sadness, I may bring joy."

Another way to work with healing crystals is to string them for someone else and either wear them while thinking of that person or give them as a gift. This can encourage you to send healing thoughts to someone who is suffering or serve as a practical reminder to keep in touch with him or her. I have a necklace with Himalayan crystal beads that I wear when any person (or pet) dear to me is ill—it makes me feel close to my friend and encourages me to offer a little extra care. My son lends me a simple green jade mala whenever I travel to connect me to him and home.

Sometimes it is helpful to pause and say the name of the person you want to send healing thoughts toward or the thing you want to heal within yourself. I wear my crystals in situations when I know there's a chance I'll be particularly exasperated. I do my best to remember to take a few slow deep breaths, hold the septarian between my fingers, mindfully appreciate the texture, and simply think "patience … patience … patience …" as deliberately as possible. It makes a difference. Is it the crystal, the pause, or the placebo? I, for one, am not going to question it because it works for me.

impermanence ZEN

The first Japanese Zen Buddhist master to teach in the United States, Sōen Shaku, wrote in 1906:

"The world is characterized by mutability and impermanence; those who do not rise above worldliness are tossed up and down in the whirlpool of passion. But those who know the constitution of things see the infinite in the finite and the supra-phenomenal in the phenomenal, and are blessed in the midst of sufferings and tribulations."

Indeed, the word "Zen" can be translated as "meditation" or a "meditative state" and if practiced with a whole heart may become a way of living in perpetual mindfulness, not choosing one experience or emotion over another but being fully with it—all of it.

This includes impermanence—not just what is, but the genuine acknowledgment that nothing will last forever. It's a straightforward yet challenging practice and one we can work with using beads that aren't designed for durability or posterity, but the opposite—transience, insubstantiality, ephemerality. By recognizing the impermanence of everything around us (including ourselves) we become more awake to the world and indeed to our lives.

creation: MY ZEN BRACELET

Most of the strands of beads in this book are meant to last, but not this one! That's why they are made of the least permanent material I could think of—paper. They're easy to make and inexpensive but they look quite lovely when they are complete.

For my paper beads, I chose to use copies of calligraphy representing two Buddhist *sutras* (texts) that were meaningful to me. You can find out how to make paper beads on pages 74–75.

"*The paper beads of my Zen bracelet remind me that nothing will last forever.*"

HOW TO MAKE PAPER BEADS

1 Collect scraps of paper to use to construct the beads. These can be arbitrary or you can imbue your scraps with symbolism via color, source, or what is printed on them. Try using pictures from magazines, old love letters, pages photocopied from treasured books, or handwritten poems or affirmations.

2 Cut the paper into long triangular strips, keeping in mind that the pointed end will be the outside of the bead. Scissors work well, but an X-Acto knife and straight-edged ruler are more accurate. For my beads, I cut triangles 6 in. (15 cm) long with a ½ in. (1 cm) base. The longer the triangle of paper, the thicker the bead.

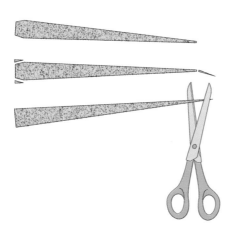

3 Snip the paper a little below the apex of the triangle so there will be a flat edge. Also, taper the triangle to the base by making a slanting cut on each side from about ½ in. (1 cm) up. This ensures that the openings at either end of your beads will be smooth once the paper has been rolled.

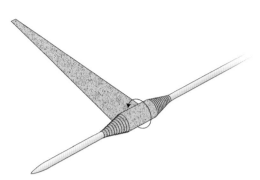

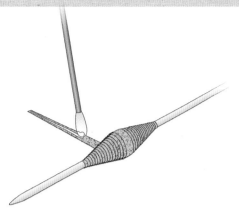

4 Roll the paper strip around a small stick, slightly larger in diameter than the string you plan to use—a thin wooden skewer, a ⅛ in. (3 mm) dowel, or a toothpick. Place the triangle's thickest part, i.e. the tapered base, against the stick first and roll the paper as tightly as possible.

5 Stop rolling when ¾ in. (2 cm) of the paper strip remains. Apply clear-drying craft glue to this narrow strip and finish rolling up the bead. Only a small amount of glue is needed—too much will mar the outer surface of the bead, destroying the image.

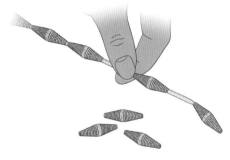

6 Continue in this way until you have enough beads, about 18 for a bracelet. Use as many sticks as necessary. For a little more (but not too much) durability, varnish the beads with an acrylic medium. Leave them on the stick while doing this. Rotate and separate the beads before the medium has completely dried so they won't get stuck together or adhere to the stick.

7 Carefully slide the beads off the stick, and then string them together on something that will hold them but not for too long. I used simple kitchen string. The look of your impermanent creation will depend on the size and color of paper you choose.

consideration: ZEN BUDDHIST MEDITATION

As you go through the steps of making and stringing your impermanent beads, consider reciting a gatha—a verse of mindfulness meant to be repeated silently or chanted in a group. In his *Manual of Zen Buddhism* (originally published in 1934), another important early transmitter of Zen from the East to the West, Daisetz Teitaro Suzuki, presented something called the "Gatha of Impermanence."

"All composite things are impermanent,
They are subject to birth and death;
Put an end to birth and death,
And there is a blissful tranquility."

Once your impermanent beads have dried, try wearing them while practicing basic Zen Buddhist meditation:

1 Find a comfortable seated position that you can hold for a long time. Many of us associate meditation with sitting in full lotus posture but the only magic about that is it is quite steady, so find the posture that is best for you—it may be on a cushion on the floor or in a chair. In general, the closer to the ground and the more symmetrical your body, the more likely it is that you will be able to hold the position for a long period of time.

2 Keeping your body centered and your back straight, place your hands in your lap, resting the less dominant hand on top of the dominant one. So, if you are right-handed, place your left hand on your right. Do this lightly—without tension—and so that the knuckles overlap.

3 Close your mouth, press your tongue against the roof of your palate, and breathe through your nose naturally—don't force or hold your breath.

4 Once you've settled into your seat and your breath, lower your gaze and count to ten, syncing each number to a cycle of inhalation and exhalation. In other words, count one, inhale then exhale, count two, inhale and exhale … Whenever your thoughts float away from your breath, return to the number one.

5 You'll find it quite difficult to reach ten, but with practice you will eventually be able to do it with ease. Once you have reached this point, let go of the numbers and simply breath—don't judge or erase thoughts or get wrapped up in them, just see them and let them go, appreciating that they are as impermanent as waves in a pond, wind among trees.

Wear your beads as a reminder of this impermanence and when they eventually deteriorate, dissolve, and disappear, you might be inspired to repeat a universal mantra that is as simple as it is powerful:

This, too, shall pass.

day of the dead MEXICO

Part of being mindful is being aware, of showing up for the entirety of life—the joyful and the sad, the beautiful and the ugly, the beginning and the end. It's what seminal American mindfulness teacher Jon Kabat-Zinn called "full catastrophe living." As he explained:

"Catastrophe ... means the poignant enormity of our life experience. It includes crises and disaster but also all the little things that go wrong and that add up. The phrase reminds us that life is always in flux, that everything we think is permanent is actually only temporary and constantly changing. This includes our ideas, our opinions, our relationships, our jobs, our possessions, our creations, our bodies, everything."

And it includes the people we love and those who guide us on our paths. Just as we commemorate births and marriages and other milestones, so we should be aware of the whole circle, even death.

We all miss somebody and Day of the Dead beads are a way to honor them. The Day of the Dead or *Dia de los Muertos* is observed on November 2 throughout Mexico to remember, connect with, and pray for friends and family members who have died. It's a holiday of grief, if you will, that evolved from an Aztec festival honoring the goddess of the afterlife, Mictecacihuatl, in tandem with teachings of Catholicism. Coinciding with Halloween and All Saints Day, Day of the Dead celebrants visit cemeteries or build memorial altars in their homes and bring gifts for the deceased, such as favorite foods, statues of saints, candles, marigolds, cigarettes, and photographs. What matters more than the actual gifts is the spirit of the things that are offered. *Calacas* and *calaveras*—skeletons and skulls—are the most representative symbols of the holiday and are created in sugar, chocolate, masks, and dolls.

On the Day of the Dead an air of revelry and humor—of life—prevails, shared by the celebrants as they tell entertaining stories about their loved ones, recount the year that has passed, and ask for advice and guidance. It's this confluence of grief and joy that I find so deeply compelling.

These multicolored ceramic skulls are a typical feature of Day of the Dead celebrations.

creation: MY DAY OF THE DEAD BEADS

There are many types of Day of the Dead beads—some literal, others abstract, and yet others relevant only to an individual. These tiny colorful skulls inspired me. In one way they're morbid, yet in another cheerful, and the pairing of these emotions can be quite meaningful as we grieve for the dead yet celebrate how we loved them.

Select beads that have a special association with someone you want to remember and remain connected with. It could be an image or color or something very specific, such as the buttons from your grandmother's wedding dress, a charm of a favorite flower or car, a birthstone, or a wooden bead that's exactly the color of your dog's fur. Then string your beads in increments that symbolize a connection to the person you're remembering—perhaps the numbers representing a birthday or anniversary or first meeting.

At a memorial service I attended, the organizers distributed strings of festive Mardi Gras beads to everyone who was there. It was a lovely gesture, keeping us all mindful of the life we were celebrating as well as the loss we shared.

"With these beads I can celebrate those I've loved as well as mourn their loss."

consideration: REMEMBERING THOSE WHOM WE'VE LOST

Artist and religion scholar Netanel Miles-Yépez wrote about celebrating the Day of the Dead every day:

"For the dead are, according to Mexican belief, always with us. We remember them daily, speak to them when we need to, and even celebrate their death-anniversaries. (A kind of "birthday in heaven!") This was something I learned very early when my *abuelita*, my grandmother, first taught me to say my prayers. She would put me to bed at night, and we would pray for my mother, my brother, my aunts, and uncles, and each of my many cousins. But when we had finished praying for the living, we would then pray for the dead ... for her mother and father, for her brothers and sisters, for my grandfather "in heaven," and for my cousin who had been murdered. Somehow, it felt as if we were fulfilling a holy purpose with these prayers, giving something necessary to the souls of the dead, and I believe I slept more peacefully because of it.

It was not until I was older that I realized that most of the people I knew did not pray for their dead. The dead were *just dead* to them, or in a kind of heaven where they did not need our prayers, or in a hell where our prayers could not help them. But my grandmother's heaven was not a place out of reach, not a place where the dead had nothing to do with us. Her heaven was a place of souls, where our ancestors and loved-ones dwelt together, a place where we could continue to speak to them, to offer them our love, and ask their help when we needed it."

1   Relate Miles-Yépez's wisdom to your experience as you think of the people you love who have passed away—it could be a family member, a hero, a spiritual teacher, mentor, or companion.
2   Put it in any context that is meaningful to you, remembering that many cultures share the tradition of honoring the dead all over the world, including Korea, Nepal, North America, Africa, and Eastern Europe.
3   As you hold your beads, repeat the names of the dead slowly, deliberately connecting with what they meant to you and how they're still in your life today. They are gone but still with you.

misbahah ISLAM

Traditionally used by Muslims as prayer beads, the misbahah, or subha, is sometimes called the Islamic rosary. These beads and their eloquent symbolism inspire people of all faiths. Misbahah are usually strings of 99 beads (or divisions thereof) used as mindfulness tools and to aid concentration for reciting the 99 "beautiful" names or attributes of God. They culminate in one elongated terminal or focal bead representing the oneness, unity, and ultimate or "essential" name of God.

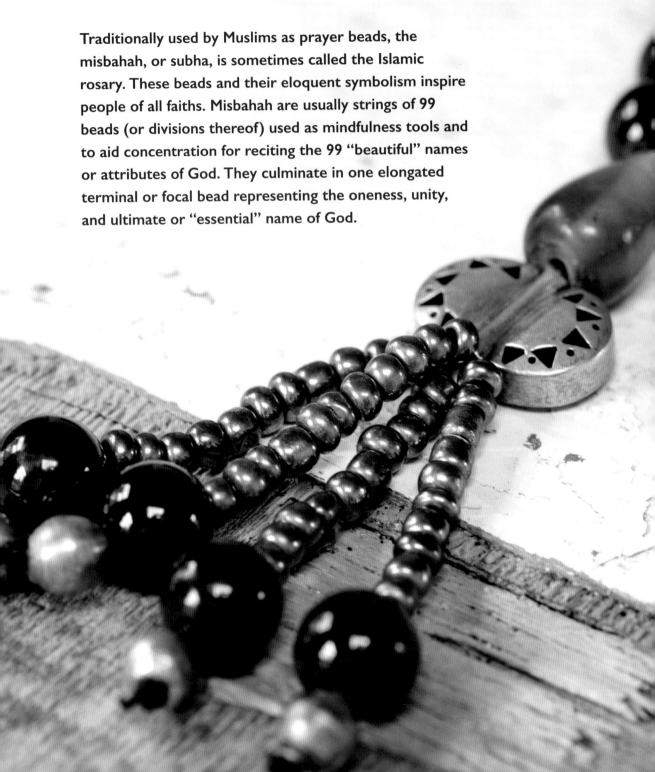

33 NAMES OF GOD

(For where to find all 99 names of God, see Websites on page 124.)

* The Merciful
* The Most Sacred
* The Embodiment of Peace
* The Infuser of Faith
* The Preserver of Safety
* The Creator
* The Evolver
* The Great Forgiver
* The All-Knowing
* The Elevating
* The Embodiment of Justice
* The Knower of Subtleties
* The Great Forgiver
* The Bountiful One
* The Watchful One
* The Responding One
* The Wise One

* The Loving One
* The Glorious One
* The All-Observing Witness
* The Embodiment of Truth
* The Originator
* The Restorer
* The Manifest
* The Hidden
* The Source of All Goodness
* The Forgiver
* The Compassionate
* The Gatherer
* The Bestower of Sufficiency
* The Prime Light
* The Provider of Guidance
* The Patient

Your understanding of God might be as Mercy, Generosity, Beneficence, Peace, Security, Sacredness, or another definition altogether, but whatever your interpretation, it's a lovely practice to hold the beads and focus on the names for what is holy as you nurture a connection with that quality.

"I use my misbahah as an aid for contemplation."

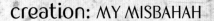

creation: MY MISBAHAH

This is one of my favorite sets of mindful beads. It's a little heavy to wear around my wrist, and not the right size, so I think of it more as an object of mindfulness than jewelry. I like to keep it as a placeholder when I'm reading or writing and have books laid out open on my desk. It gives the process of the work and the words a sense of gravitas and higher purpose.

Misbahah beads can be made from lapis lazuli, terra-cotta, carnelian, sandalwood, rosewood, ivory, pearls, amber, hard plastic, olive seeds, or date pits from the holy city of Mecca (the birthplace of the Prophet Muhammad). I chose carnelian beads because I was drawn to the heft and the deep red color. The metallic beads used for the four-strand tassel were ones I had. I liked the feel of them and the contrast between the stone and metal. The focal beads are a silver one I had been saving for a special project that just seemed right, and a smoky glass teardrop that evoked mystery for me.

For the main part, I strung 33 beads on two-stranded thread (the tradition is to go around three times to recite all 99 names of God). Stringing this project was a challenge because the beads were heavy and it was not just a simple loop—I also needed to create four tassels to hang below the focal beads for the misbahah theme. The best way I could do this was to work up from the end of the first tassel, carrying on to create the main (33-bead) loop, and then work down to make a second tassel.

So, I started with the metal bead at the end of the first tassel, added a carnelian and then 11 small beads, passed the thread through the two focal beads, on through the 33 carnelians, and back through the focal beads, adding another 11 small beads, a carnelian, and the end bead to make a second tassel. The other two tassels were created on a shorter separate thread that was tied beneath the focal beads, using a square knot.

consideration: CONNECTING TO THE DIVINE

The word *misbahah* comes from the root meaning to "exalt" or "praise," and these beads can be used to be mindful of, celebrate, and appreciate God with and within all and each of us. As you hold your misbahah in your hand, sit quietly and spend time with the sensation of the weight and form of each bead. Move them slowly and deliberately through your fingers. As you clasp one bead at a time, recite a word or name that connects you to the Divine. After you do so, you might want to conclude by contemplating or saying these inspiring words from a prayer attributed to the Prophet Muhammad:

"Light on my right hand
and light on my left hand
and light above me
and light below me ...
... increase the light within me.
... give me light
and illuminate me."

numbering days CHINA

Since childhood I've been fascinated by abacuses—the Chinese calculating tool used to tally numbers by moving beads along horizontal sticks. The first Chinese abacuses appeared during the second century BCE and some historians believe that the practice of counting prayers by using beads—malas, rosaries, misbahah—originated with the abacus.

There's something so satisfying about the form and heft of Chinese abacus beads, and they seemed perfect for wearing on wrists, so I wanted to come up with a mindful application for them—that was the inspiration for Numbering Days beads. You can use them to commemorate an anniversary, a first date, a birthday, vacation, reunion, or a graduation—any sort of milestone.

You can also use them to remind you of, or connect you with, a special or mystical number. All cultures associate certain numbers with fortune and misfortune in one way or another—think of "lucky" seven and "unlucky" 13. Sometimes special numbers are the dates associated with important events, personal landmarks, or something like a solstice or the heeding of the Ides of March. Chinese culture is no different and many numbers are traditionally auspicious or inauspicious.

* Two is a lucky number because "good things come in pairs."
* Eight is considered especially lucky as are series of eights, so you might want to string your mindful beads in increments of eight. Also, the Buddha's birthday is April 8.
* Nine is associated with royalty and the Emperor of China, whose robes often incorporated nine dragons.
* Avoid increments of four or numbers that include four, such as 14, because these are associated with death.

When you're coming up with ideas for your Numbering Days beads, you might refer to the *I Ching* or *Book of Changes*, which is the ancient Chinese divination text that has provided insights into self-understanding, poetry, art, life, and even scientific thought for centuries. Many versions are available at bookstores and libraries, and on websites (see page 124). In the book, you can learn about a process for throwing three coins or 50 yarrow sticks to form hexagrams (a combination of six broken and unbroken lines) and consulting the corresponding I Ching number for predictions and insights. I like just to read random passages and find the wisdom associated with certain numbers in order to make my own connections. For example:

* 1—*Khien*: what is great and originating, penetrating, helpful, correct, and steady. A sign of beginnings and remembering our foundations.
* 11—*Thâi*: that which comes and goes, symbolizing good fortune, progress, and success. A number that indicates overcoming adversity to reach a goal.
* 17—*Î*: if we do the work, we'll reap rewards. If we focus on our true purpose, we'll achieve it.

Of course, as with all mindful beads, in the end, it is up to you to decide what resonates with meaning.

Ancient Chinese coins are used to encourage good fortune.

CHINESE ZODIAC

Another possibility for your beads is to take a look at the Chinese Zodiac, which differs from the Western solar one. It's based on birth year rather than month, and the symbolism and characteristics are based on animals instead of mythological characters and beings. You might want to incorporate a number related to your birth year and a bead with the corresponding animal's symbol.

Rat	1924, 1936, 1948, 1960, 1972, 1984, 1996, 2008, 2020
Ox or Cow	1925, 1937, 1949, 1961, 1973, 1985, 1997, 2009, 2021
Tiger	1926, 1938, 1950, 1962, 1974, 1986, 1998, 2010, 2022
Rabbit	1939, 1951, 1963, 1975, 1987, 1999, 2011, 2023
Dragon	1928, 1940, 1952, 1964, 1976, 1988, 2000, 2012, 2024
Serpent or Snake	1929, 1941, 1953, 1965, 1977, 1989, 2001, 2013, 2025
Horse	1930, 1942, 1954, 1966, 1978, 1990, 2002, 2014, 2026
Goat, Ram, or Sheep	1931, 1943, 1955, 1967, 1979, 1991, 2003, 2015, 2027
Monkey	1932, 1944, 1956, 1968, 1980, 1992, 2004, 2016, 2028
Rooster or Chicken	1945, 1957, 1969, 1981, 1993, 2005, 2017, 2029
Dog	1934, 1946, 1958, 1970, 1982, 1994, 2006, 2018, 2030
Boar or Pig	1947, 1959, 1971, 1983, 1995, 2007, 2019, 2031

creation: MY NUMBERING DAYS BRACELET

I bought an abacus on eBay, which was not expensive despite the nice wooden beads. Fortunately, I was able to disassemble it quite easily so that I could use the beads for my Numbering Days bracelets and save the sticks and frame for other projects. One of the bracelets was going to be a New Year's gift, so I used one bead for January (the first month), one bead for the first day, and 17 beads for the year—January 1, 2017. Also, lucky numbers 9 and 8 add up to 17, and I like the message of the I Ching 17. The other bracelet is made with 21 beads, based solely on size. I incorporated a Chinese coin that I'd found because it made me think of I Ching divination coins.

I chose to string the beads on red elastic, and I also selected a red imitation cinnabar focal bead and two red spacer beads because red is known to stand for good fortune, luck, and joy in China. It's the color of New Year's firecrackers and the envelopes that gifts of money come in. Also, the large red bead can stand for "one" in I Ching terminology.

"My bracelets are made from wooden abacus beads."

The beads are black because the abacus I liked was made with black beads, but I was fascinated to learn that black is considered a neutral color—the color of water—and, according to the I Ching, associated with heaven.

The beads are large with wide holes, so the red elastic had to be quite thick and was easy to work with. I wrapped a piece of cellophane tape around the end to make threading easier and so the elastic wouldn't fray. I tied the bracelets off with a square knot and then used a drop of strong glue to anchor and hide the knot inside one of the beads.

consideration: REMEMBERING SPECIAL MOMENTS

As you wear or give away your Numbering Days beads, use them as a reminder of the event, milestone, or number they stand for. Take the time to appreciate the experience, be mindful of the moment, and remember that time is fluid. Consider this wisdom from the ancient Chinese philosopher Confucius, who taught:

"What are the words of Heaven?
The four seasons pass, the hundred things bear life ...

The course and nature of things is such that
What was in front is now behind ... "

love letters ZULU

The Roman poet Ovid wrote, "Ring, to encircle my beautiful girl's finger, appreciated only in terms of the giver's love, go as a dear gift!" Ancient Sumerian, Greek, and Egyptian royalty were buried with gifts of crowns and necklaces to enjoy in the afterlife. Gifts of beads as tokens of affection and connection between beloveds is probably as old as jewelry itself. Think of engagement rings, and exchanging wedding bands, using the words, "With this ring I thee wed." Jewelry is often used to symbolize promises and as a tangible emblem of reward or spiritual connection. That's the idea behind these beaded bracelets, inspired by Zulu love letters.

Traditional Zulu beadwork incorporates meaning and messages within it.

The Zulu people of South Africa have a long history with beads. They decorated garments and created ornaments using ostrich shell disks until glass beads were introduced by European traders, missionaries, and travelers in the fifteenth century. By the nineteenth century, beads had really taken off as a part of Zulu culture, and were treasured by royalty. The use of brightly colored beads evolved into love letters or tokens—woven squares or strips of beadwork patterns containing secret messages. These are now most often made by teenaged girls, depicting elaborate and beautiful geometric patterns, such as herringbone, a series of triangles, or motifs from nature.

What is most fascinating to me about Zulu love letters is that every element of these intricate creations has meaning—the symmetric patterns, which are read from the center, the relationship between the color of beads and the colors themselves. These meanings change over time and vary between communities. In one example, where the Zulu word for lavender is also the name of a species of violet-gray dove, the expression associated with this color bead is "*Liyajabula ijuba lone licosha izinihlamvu emnyango knewu*," which loosely translates as "I am envious of the dove that gathers the seeds near the door of your mother's hut because it can be close to you."

In the list below I've combined and simplified the color associations I've found in a variety of sources, including a reference written by Zulu Princess Constance Magogo kaDinuzulu (1900–1984), a noted musician and artist, and the daughter of King Dinuzulu kaCetshwayo. It's important to note that, except for white, bead colors have both negative and positive connotations. If a white bead is strung next to a bead of another color, that bead is interpreted with a positive meaning.

COLOR ASSOCIATIONS

* **Black**—grief, loneliness, I hear you love another, I miss you, darkness, disappointment, sorrow
* **Blue**—faithfulness, fidelity, ill-feeling, a request—"If I were a bird I would soar through blue skies to you."
* **Brown**—"My love for you is like the soil that gives rise to new beginnings."
* **Green**—love-sickness, jealousy, domestic bliss, contentment, sickness, discord—"I have become as thin as newly sprouting saplings and grasses as I pine for you."

* **Pink**—abject poverty, lost money, lack of funds for a dowry
* **Red**—passionate love, longing, intense emotion—"My heart is so full of love that it bleeds for you."
* **Striped beads**—distrust, blame, cheating
* **Turquoise**—impatience, diminishing hope for the relationship
* **White**—true and spiritual love, hope, purity, cleanliness, vision, goodness, fortune, happiness, children
* **Yellow**—money or the lack of it

The forms of the beading patterns matter as well:

* **A triangle** stands for female
* **An inverted triangle** stands for male
* **A diamond shape**—two triangles joined at the base—stands for a married woman
* **An hourglass shape**—two triangles connected at the point—stands for a married man

creation: MY LOVE LETTER BRACELETS

The bracelets I made reflect a simplified version of the love letters. I combined this with the idea of LDR or "long-distance relationship" beads that has become quite popular. It is the trend of giving a bracelet to a friend, partner, or love interest to wear when you're apart.

I strung the beads on very thin elastic, using simple seed beads to make two sets of three bracelets—one for myself and one to give away. I wanted them to be light for travel and so that they could be worn with other jewelry. The colors blue and white remind the wearers to be mindful of true and spiritual love and faith in one another.

"I encoded the message 'I love you' into these two sets of beads."

The white beads make a very simple triangle when the three blue bracelets are stacked (and vice versa). This is to reflect the triangles used in Zulu love letters, but also my own coded way of communicating. When my son was very small and I dropped him off at school or he was drifting back to sleep after a bad dream, I'd squeeze his hand three times as a "secret" way of communicating the three words: "I love you."

consideration: SHARING WITH LOVED ONES

String the Zulu Love-Letter beads with someone you care for—a person whom you miss when you're apart. Share the significance of the color and patterns with your friend, child, or partner. You could do this before a long separation, as closure after resolving a disagreement, or as a private token of commitment or shared purpose. Mindfully make the bracelet for the other person, and have them make yours for you as you both consider the meaning you have given to the beads.

As you do so, you could contemplate or repeat the Zulu saying "*Umuntu ngumuntu ngabantu*," which translates to mean, "A person is the person they are because of the people around them." You could acknowledge one another's *Ubuntu*, which, according to Archbishop Desmond Tutu in his book *No Future without Forgiveness* means "My humanity is caught up, is inextricably bound up, in yours." Think about speaking this beautiful sentiment of altruism, love, and mindfulness as you give the beads to someone you care about. What a wonderful thing to meditate on each time you wear your Zulu Love-Letter beads!

An alternative is to recite this beautiful South African proverb together, or add it as a note with a gift of the beads:

Love, like rain, does not choose the grass on which it falls.

shiva's eyes HINDUISM

The Shiva's Eyes necklace is another traditional mala, but unlike the Buddhist-influenced Moon and Stars, this one takes its imagery from Hinduism. As with Buddhist malas, Hindu malas have 108 beads and are used to count prayers or breaths and focus contemplation.

In Hinduism the number 108 has yet another interesting association—in Hindu or Vedic astrology it is considered sacred because of the nine planets traveling through twelve constellations or signs of the zodiac. The system is a bit different from the Western astrology that most of us are familiar with. Vedic astrology charts *graha*— a word rooted in *grahana*, which means "eclipse"—because of the powers that heavenly bodies have to eclipse and pull our minds. The heavenly bodies in question are listed in the chart below.

VEDIC ASTROLOGICAL ASSOCIATIONS

Surya or Ravi	Sun	**Shukra**	Venus
Chandra or Soma	Moon	**Shani**	Saturn
Mangala	Mars	**Rahu**	Dragon's Head, the northernmost point node of the moon, where its path intersects with the sun in their orbits
Budha	Mercury		
Guru	Jupiter, the master of all *grahas*	**Ketu**	Dragon's Tail, the southernmost point node of the moon, where its path intersects with the sun in their orbits

Although they are not planets, moons, or stars, both Rahu and Ketu are sometimes called "shadow planets" because their effect on humanity is a result of their light and its presence and absence.

Hindu malas have 108 beads and are often made of rudraksha seeds.

creation: MY SHIVA'S EYES NECKLACE

Since many Hindu malas are made with rudraksha seeds, I wanted to work with those. They grow on the utrasum bead tree or *Elaeocarpus ganitrus*—an evergreen tree found in the foothills of the Himalayas, southeast Asia, Nepal, Indonesia, New Guinea, Australia, and even Hawaii. I selected smaller seeds for my necklace and I love the pebbly texture. They are readily available online and at most craft stores, especially those that specialize in Asian products.

It turns out rudraksha seeds are sacred to the god Shiva, who is said to have worn them in garlands. The Sanskrit roots of the word are *rudra*, a synonym for Shiva—one of the principal deities in Hinduism—and *aksa* meaning teardrops, for the tears of joy Shiva shed after destroying demons, tears which nurtured a rudraksha tree. They are also commonly called the "eyes of Shiva." The rough texture of the seeds is said to symbolize the difficulties of life—our demons.

It goes even deeper than that. When, in his book *Shiva: The Wild God of Power and Ecstasy*, German ethnologist and anthropologist Wolf-Dieter Storl asked a Hindu holy

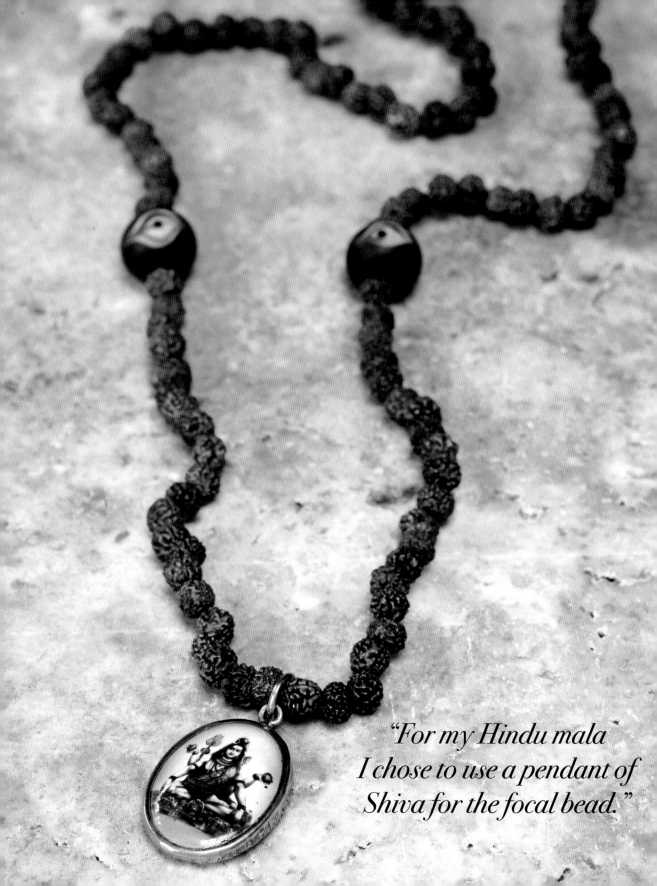

*"For my Hindu mala
I chose to use a pendant of
Shiva for the focal bead."*

man living in the Nepalese jungle about the meaning of rudraksha seeds, he was told that "all our wishes, thoughts, words, and deeds are like the seeds of a plant sown into fertile ground. They might rest there in the dark, invisible and forgotten, but sooner or later they will sprout, grow tall, flower, and finally shoot to seed. Rather than sowing these seeds of suffering anew, one can string them up and wear them as a sign that one's karma has ended."

In India, rudraksha seeds are categorized, studied, and collected in the way the French do with wine or a chef might treat varieties of salt or vinegar. The value and rarity of rudraksha seeds is based upon the form of the seed—the more facets there are or the rarer the shape, the greater the value and desirability. Some are sold for as much as fine diamonds.

The facets are called *mukhis* and each one represents a spiritual aspect or God. The seeds in my mala are five-faced, or *Panchmukhi*, which are the most common and evoke the presence of Shiva, partly because five is the number sacred to him. It is said that the seeds will help the wearer conquer and transcend their troubles. Who doesn't need that at some point in their lives?

When I discovered the connection between rudraksha seeds and Shiva, I decided to make this god of destruction, transformation, and the resulting creation the theme for my mindful beads. According to Wolf-Dieter Storl, "Shiva is not only the god of gods, but of the demons as well. He embodies the primal oneness, before the world divided itself into the divine and demonic forces." Perhaps that makes him the god of our innermost selves. I thought the concept of wholeness that Shiva represents makes a powerful connection with the idea of the circle, which has no beginning or end, like a string of mindful beads.

Although Hindu malas are traditionally made from natural materials, I've added a fabricated element—the focal or guru bead. I did this because I wanted to stay with my theme and use a remarkable Shiva amulet I found. If you look at this pendant, or other images of Shiva, you'll see that he is depicted with a third eye. It is said that opening his third eye annihilates desire and evokes a deeper kind of seeing or vision. I put a larger rudraksha seed opposite the guru bead to symbolize this.

The two beads I used to offset the focal bead aren't traditional Hindu mala beads either, but I selected them because they are eyes. These are from Java and called *jatim*. They are hand inlaid glass and a play on the Eastern Mediterranean evil eye, a symbol that protects its wearer from bad luck or injury. They seemed to fit my theme.

consideration: MEDITATING ON WONDER

As you sit quietly and meditate holding or wearing your Shiva's Eyes beads, consider this line from Wolf-Dieter Storl concerning a manifestation of Shiva:

> "Everything is divine and worthy of worship, though there is no compulsion to worship it."

Or perhaps this quote about milkweed pods from one of my favorites—American nineteenth-century author and transcendentalist Henry David Thoreau—who may have never seen a rudraksha bead, but knew a great deal about seeds, seeing, and the promise in the cycles of nature:

> "I am interested in every such venture the autumn sends forth. And for this end these silken streamers have been perfecting themselves all summer, snugly packed in this light chest, a perfect adaptation to this end—a prophecy not only of the fall, but of future springs. Who could believe in [other] prophecies... that the world would end this summer, while one milkweed with faith matured its seeds?"

vision beads SHAMANISM

A shaman is a person who can connect with the spirit world to receive insights, healing, or energetic powers, often by entering an altered state of consciousness, sometimes called a vision quest. This could be achieved through forms of ritual and meditation or by consuming mind-altering substances. Shamanism crosses all cultures from Mongolia to Morocco, the Hopi Nation to Hawaii, Australia to the Amazon. Mircea Eliade, the twentieth-century Romanian religion scholar and author described a shaman thus:

"...the shaman is also a magician and medicine man; he is believed to cure, like all doctors, and to perform miracles of the fakir type, like all magicians whether primitive or modern. But beyond this, he is a psychopomp [soul guide], and he may also be a priest, mystic, and poet."

The possibilities for Vision Beads are as myriad as the societies and philosophies that shamanism spans, but along with a belief in a supernatural power that organizes and governs the universe, all types of shamanism share the transformative connection to the natural world—plants, cosmic phenomena, and especially animals.

Helpful spirits are said to draw on the abilities of "power" animals—hunting like a jaguar becomes discernment, wiliness like a snake becomes problem-solving. Pretty much every animal has a myth or spiritual capability within one culture or another, and we can all find one to adopt, which will inspire us and infuse our dreams. It's a personal thing—which animal *feels* right for you? Which one has characteristics you like about yourself or want to work on? On the following pages are some suggested animals from a variety of sources.

ANIMAL GUIDES

bear	healing, gentle strength, and connection to the earth
deer	grace, beauty, and agility
badger	deep wisdom
mouse	humility and discovery
coyote	shadow self, intelligence, and ingenuity
buffalo	power and abundance
lion	loyalty, dignity, and strength
cheetah	speed, self-esteem, and vision
hippopotamus	rebirth and renewal
crocodile	creative power and realized goals
elephant	reaching goals
camel	inner strength
beaver	industry and care for the environment, the subconscious
turtle	service, motherhood, and generosity
dolphin	communication, intelligence, whimsy
whale	soul memory and depth of understanding

pelican	recovery from loss and charity in abundance
frog	cleansing, rebirth, interconnection of all life
spider	creation and finding meaning in patterns
ant	hard work and persistence
butterfly	transformation and joy
bee	appreciation for the sweetness of life
eagle	family and relationships, connection to the Divine, courage
hawk	illumination, creativity, and truth
crow	messenger between spiritual and mortal world
owl	alchemy, freedom, and messenger of omens
hummingbird	protection on long journeys and love
cat	self-love and care, independence, intuition
dog	loyalty, power, and devotion

You could select one or many of these spirit animals for your Vision Beads—the more you read, the more interesting connections you will discover. Alternatively, you could use specific attributes, such as feathers, teeth, fur, or eye color, to represent them.

"*The three turtles in my vision beads symbolize generosity.*"

creation: MY VISION BEADS

I chose turtles for one of my two Vision Bead bracelets because they symbolize generosity and I connect that to gratitude, which I want to be conscious of, especially as a mother. As I researched, I learned that turtles also signify life's continuous cycle of birth, persistence, and regeneration. Native American Ojibway lore tells of a turtle spirit called *mikinak* that solves problems and answers questions, and a Senecan legend says the Great Tree of Life grows from the shell of a turtle. Hindu mythology tells of the Earth being supported by four elephants who stand on the shell of a turtle.

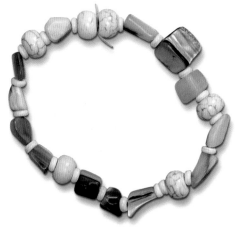

These things made the turtle beads especially meaningful to me and I chose to have three of them because three is such a significant number—the triangle, the Christian trinity, the Hindu Tridevi or three goddesses, and the Buddhist Three Jewels (the Buddha, the teachings, and the Buddhist community).

Seven is a mystical number in so many cultures—seen as "perfect" and associated with such things as the seven days of creation, seven chakras, seven levels of consciousness, and seven heavens. So, I strung seven beads of wood and metal between the turtles. Wood and metal are natural materials that seemed right.

My second set of Vision Beads was much simpler. I strung shells as well as beads that look like bones and teeth (but are a stone composite). I thought this balanced the turtle bracelet well and evoked nature in an unpolished way.

I strung both sets of beads on sturdy elastic and hid the square knots in a bead with a drop of glue.

consideration: YOUR SHAMANIC VISION QUEST

Shamanism spans so many cultures and countries that many meditative practices could be connected to it. You could try this one.

1　Find a quiet place in your environment and in yourself. Holding your Vision Beads, take a few deep breaths and as you settle into the inhalation and the exhalation, focus on the animal (or one of the animals) you have chosen for your beads and ask yourself some questions:

* What quality does the animal embody for you?
* How can you manifest that in your life?
* How does that reveal the interconnection of all beings in the universe?
* What can you do to protect what the animal represents within you and the world?

2　From there, you could try a modified version of a shamanic vision quest. In essence, it's a meditation using imagery with a clear beginning and end—a mind journey. Once you've stilled your thoughts and connected in a deep way to your spirit animal, close your eyes and picture the animal. What do you see? Look for details of appearance and behavior.

3　Imagine that the animal is guiding you somewhere. Where do you go? What happens there? Do you receive a message? How can you relate what you've seen or imagined to your real-life issues and concerns?

These practices can be fascinating and can illuminate challenges or answer questions, but a vision quest can be even simpler. Sit quietly on the sofa with your dog or cat and calmly pet it. Really pay attention to the animal. Just be with it—really be—and consider what it's thinking. What does the animal dream of? What qualities does it have that can guide you in your life? Your spirit guide may have been with you all along.

worry beads GREECE

Long before fidget spinners arrived on the scene, people diminished anxiety and stayed focused using komboloi, or worry beads. They are a familiar sight and sound (*click-click click-click*) in Greece and the countries surrounding the Mediterranean Sea. People young and old carry komboloi with them and slide the beads across the thread, often unconsciously, while they're walking, working, talking, and waiting.

The word "komboloi" comes from *kombos* (knot) and *logio* (collection) or *leo* (say). It is believed that the Eastern Orthodox monks of Greece's Mount Athos, the Holy Mountain, knotted string in increments to mark their prayers, or made beads from whatever was at hand, and these evolved into the Greek worry bead. Nobody seems to know how it caught on from there.

Worry beads come in a variety of colors and are hugely popular in Greece.

The repetitive motion of fidgeting with the beads does seem to relieve stress, and there is neuroscientific research to support this. According to the American Psychological Association's website, University College London researchers "found that viewers who performed a visuospatial task while they watched a distressing video suffered fewer intrusive memories in the following week than viewers who performed a verbal task." Such a "visuospatial" task would be employing worry beads (or any sort of hand-held kinetic item, even a lump of clay) to help the user focus and filter out negative external stimuli.

Another theory is that the relief brought by fidgeting with komboloi is the result of stimulating acupressure points. According to Chinese medicine, pressure points related to the head and brain are located in the thumbs and fingers and are especially a trigger release for nervousness. Either way, there is something quite addictive about it and once you start handling them, it's hard to stop!

"My worry beads are made from obsidian."

creation: MY WORRY BEADS

Some sources say you should string 33 beads, others recommend 23, and still others say any prime number (that is one that is divisible only by itself, such as 17) to make a komboloi, but all agree that no matter how many beads it should be an odd number along with a fixed "priest" bead and a tassel. Ultimately, the length of the strand depends on the size of your hand.

Although komboloi are most often made from amber, amber resin, or coral, they can be made from any material. I chose flat oval golden-sheen obsidian for my worry beads because it felt right in my hand and I liked the color. Use something that won't break (so avoid glass) or wear out (also avoid pearls or painted wood—unless you want a worn effect).

I used 15 beads, because I wanted something small enough to put in my pocket, and left a space of about four fingers' width between the worry beads and the priest beads, stringing them on sturdy silk cord that will hold up to a lot of handling. The space between the main beads and priest beads is to allow room for you to move them around and fidget.

Instead of a priest bead and tassel I used three different-sized beads at the end of my komboloi to avoid the tangle of the tassel and because I liked how the weight of these focal beads balanced the worry beads.

consideration: SEARCHING FOR CALM

To use your komboloi, start at the focal beads and slide one of the worry beads along the thread to meet it—click, repeat, click, repeat, click, repeat ad infinitum, staying mindful of your beads and using this focus to help percolate and process whatever might be making you anxious.

In his poignant memoir about his quest to understand worry beads—*The Komboloi and Its History*—Aris Evangelinos, co-founder of the Komboloi Museum in Argolida, Greece wrote:

> "Whenever I met someone with a komboloi in hand ... I always asked the same standard question: why this person had a komboloi, and what he did with it. I always got the same answers: because I like it ... to pass the time ... because I've given up smoking ... because I like to stroke its beads and hear its sound ... because I'm in a bad temper ... out of habit, out of boredom.
>
> "No one, however, could explain how man and komboloi could be so closely bound and live ... together in such a strong, indissoluble relationship ... without flagging in the continuous flow of time ..."

After traveling the world to find the answer to this secret, Evangelinos ultimately realized it was that the never-ending circle of worry beads connects the user with infinity. So, whether you use your komboloi to ease the stress of the moment or to put yourself within the context of the vastness of the universe, you will find that they are a reliable and outstanding mindfulness tool.

earth rosary NATURE

Christians have used prayer beads since the third century, when ascetics and hermits in Egypt and Syria—the desert fathers and mothers—carried pebbles in their pockets to count their prayers. Sacred-bead use has continued to evolve among people of all faiths.

Although most Westerners are familiar with the Catholic rosary, less well known is the non-denominational set of prayer beads called the Earth Rosary. This devotional tool for people of any faith is to help us appreciate and connect to the Earth, and perhaps renew our determination to attend to and protect our climate and environment. The Earth Rosary comprises four sets of 13 beads representing the 13 weeks in each of the four seasons, adding up to 52 weeks in a year.

creation: MY EARTH ROSARY

When I made my Earth Rosary, I sought a material that was very simple and felt good in my hands. I also wanted something natural, so I chose smooth wooden beads and strung them in four sets of 13, adding up to 52, separating each set with spacer beads.

The colors reflect nature—ivory, gray, black, and, of course, green.

I added a tree charm because trees are a constant throughout the seasons, a symbol of the connection between heaven and earth, the sacred and the everyday. I strung the beads loosely so there would be extra string because I wanted to use the Earth Rosary more as a mindfulness practice object than as something to wear.

"The colors of my Earth Rosary reflect nature."

INSPIRATION FROM NATURE

You might want to create your Earth Rosary from fancier materials, or you could turn to nature for your beads. Try using:

* acorn caps
* jingle shells (bivalve mollusks)
* tiny pinecones
* berries (the less juicy the better—fleshy ones tend to rot)
* small pieces of driftwood

A string of shell beads.

Acorn caps.

consideration: APPRECIATING THE EARTH

Go outdoors and find a spot to sit in nature, or, if that's not possible, look out of the window at something green. Take a deep breath and be mindful of your connection to the Earth, to all of creation, to the universe. Remember that just as we depend on the natural world for sustenance and inspiration, the natural world relies on us for protection. As you foster this connection, consider reciting these lines from Vietnamese Zen Buddhist teacher Thich Nhat Hanh, a mantra to repeat with each bead as they move fluidly through your fingers:

> "Water flows over these hands.
> May I use them skillfully
> to preserve our precious planet."

Instead, you might like to contemplate your gratitude for the Earth and all that it provides. These words from *The Book of Common Prayer* can be inspiring.

> "... thank you for making the earth fruitful,
> so that it might produce what is needed for life:
> Bless those who work in the fields;
> give us seasonable weather;
> and grant that we may all share the fruits of the earth,
> rejoicing in your goodness... "

Or maybe, like the desert mothers and fathers, you will choose to practice hesychasm—from the Greek "to be still"—a practice of silent and ceaseless prayer. Find that sweet spot where prayer connects to meditation within you, and whenever you drift away from it, resettle your consciousness upon your Earth Rosary. Allow it to remind you of your appreciation for the Earth and interconnection with all beings and the Divine.

luck and protection
COVERING YOUR BASES

There is a famous story that Niels Henrik David Bohr (1885–1962), the Nobel prize-winning physicist who developed the model for the atom, kept a horseshoe hanging above his door. When someone asked the internationally respected scientist if he believed the horseshoe brought him luck, Dr Bohr replied, "No! I certainly do not believe in it. However, I have observed that it works even when you don't."

Every culture has a lucky charm, color, or symbol. Why not include some of your favorites in a string of beads? They could be personal, such as beads the color of your lucky socks, a number that has particular significance, such as a child's birth date, or a bead or trinket from a place where you experienced tremendous good fortune. Otherwise, you could look through the list below for inspiration. I used many of them in my own lucky necklace (pictured opposite), explained in further detail on page 120.

GOOD-LUCK SYMBOLS AND CHARMS

There are all sorts of objects and well-known images that are said to bring luck:
* **anchor**—for mooring in stormy times
* **ankh**—the Ancient Egyptian symbol for life
* **angels**—especially guardian angels
* **bells**—like the ones rung on auspicious occasions in Buddhist temples
* **brooms**—a new broom is thought to bring luck to a new home
* **coins**—such as pennies, sixpence, I Ching coins (see page 86), American Mercury dime, or coins that are minted in a birth, or special, year
* **coral *cornicello* horn**—a traditional Italian amulet thought to repel the evil eye
* **dice**—especially combining to make lucky numbers such as seven
* **eggs**—a symbol of renewed life
* **horseshoes**—perhaps because the iron from which they are made was once considered to be lucky

- **keys**—for opening doors and unlocking obstacles
- **milagro**—Mexican folk charms used for healing purposes
- **stars**—for wishing
- **sport insignias**—to bring luck to your favorite team
- **wishbones**

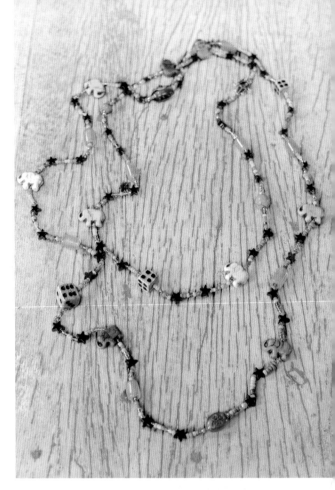

Religious medallions are sometimes symbols of good luck:
- **Saint Cecilia**—Christian patron of musicians and other performers
- **Saint Christopher**—Christian protector of travelers and children
- **cross**—symbol of connection to the holy and the universe
- **happy or laughing Buddha**—bringer of good fortune and contentment
- **Ganesh**—Hindu elephant-headed god of wisdom and new beginnings, and the remover of obstacles

A number of crystals, stones, and gems are said to bring good fortune. **Jade**, for example, also known as the "Stone of Heaven," brings luck and protection according to feng shui. The imperial gem of ancient China is believed to attract love and prosperity, and even ward off evil spirits.

Do you have a favorite color? It might be lucky, too...
- **blue**—a lucky color in many cultures, from turquoise donkey beads in Iran and the Indigo clothes of the Taureg people, to bright blue evil-eye amulets in Turkey, Greece, and throughout the Middle East
- **gold**—invites abundance and prosperity for many cultures
- **purple**—the color of royalty

* **red**—signifies a gift of good fortune in China

Specific body parts can be symbolic, such as **hands of Fatima** (*hamsa*), which are believed to bring good fortune and happiness. Eyes in particular often have special meanings:

* **eye of Providence**—often in a triangle, it stands for being watched over by God
* **eye of Horus**—Ancient Egyptian symbol of power, royalty, and protection
* **evil eye talisman** (pictured above right)—guarding you from enemies and adversity
* **eyes of Shiva**—for protection by the Hindu deity

Many rare and not so rare sights in nature are said to bring luck:

* **four-leafed clover**—the leaves are said to stand for faith, hope, love, and luck
* **shamrock** (pictured right)—a three-leafed clover, considered to be lucky in Ireland
* **bamboo**—used in feng shui to invite luck and good fortune
* **chili pepper**—another feng shui talisman
* **dandelion**—gone to seed for wishing
* **lotus**—the lovely blossom emerging from muddy water symbolizes beauty and the overcoming of adversity despite circumstances
* **peach**—associated with longevity in several Asian cultures

Finally, certain animals and other fauna can be auspicious:

* **bees**—symbols of industry, wisdom, and immortality
* **carp or koi**—good fortune in Chinese culture
* **cowrie shells**—African symbols of spiritual and monetary prosperity

* **crickets**—according to English writer Charles Dickens (1812–1870), "To have a Cricket on the Hearth, is the luckiest thing in all the world!"
* **dolphins**—since the time of the Ancient Greeks, a dolphin has been seen as a helper and guide
* **doves**—universal symbols of peace
* **eagle feathers**—sacred to many Native American cultures, they represent strength
* **elephants** (pictured right)—evoking the Hindu god Ganesh, and positive energy in feng shui

* **foo dogs**—although called "dogs," these Chinese guardians are actually lions
* **Japanese origami cranes**—the belief is that a thousand of them will make a wish come true
* **ladybugs**—said to grant wishes
* **Mandarin ducks**—which represent luck in marriage in Asian cultures
* **moon rabbits**—the Asian interpretation of the "man in the moon" image
* **pigs**—especially the three-legged chanchito charms from Chile
* **rabbit's foot**—a folk magic charm in the British Isles and American South
* **ravens**—a connection to the spirit world in many myths
* **roosters**—especially lucky in Chinese astrology
* **scarab beetles**—recreated as protection amulets by the Ancient Egyptians
* **swans**—said to bring luck in love because they mate for life
* **toads and frogs**—symbols of abundance, particularly in Asian cultures
* **tortoises**—emblems of resolve, persistence, and longevity in many cultures

creation:
MY LUCKY NECKLACE

I think it is reasonable to say that luck is subjective, so choose whatever works for you. I like the random quality of the necklace I made. I used green as a theme, since it is the color of trees and growth and has always felt lucky to me, and separated every larger charm with beads in increments of seven—a lucky number in many cultures. Among them I put:

* **stars**, because who doesn't want to wish on them?
* pieces of **Chinese jade**
* a **shamrock**
* pieces of **turquoise**
* "lucky" **dice**
* **elephants**
* an **evil-eye repelling charm** in green instead of traditional blue
* a *hamsa* hand

"My necklace has a green theme—a lucky color, and the color of growth."

consideration:
CONTEMPLATING THE NATURE OF LUCK

As you wear your beads, open yourself up to luck and welcome it. Who knows how much of it comes from within us and how much from the universe? Perhaps you agree with the American poet Emily Dickinson (1830–1886), who wrote:

Luck is Not Chance

Luck is not chance—
It's Toil—
Fortune's expensive smile
Is earned—
The Father of the Mine
Is that old fashioned Coin
We spurned—

Or maybe the Swedish proverb:

Luck never gives; it only lends.

Or this traditional Irish good luck blessing:

May joy and peace surround you,
May contentment latch your door,
May happiness be with you now
and bless you forevermore!

I tend to stand by this old saying:

Luck is what happens when preparation
meets opportunity.

bibliography

publications

Aikman, Z. Susanne. *A primer, the art of Native American beadwork: with projects*, 1990; Denver, Colorado; Morning Flower Press

Arettam, Joanna, *Dharma Beads: Making and Using Your Own Buddhist Malas*, 2000; North Clarendon, Vermont; Journey Editions, Tuttle Publishing

Beckwith, Martha Warren, *Folk-games of Jamaica*, 1922; Poughkeepsie, New York; Vassar College

Berkers, Ewald, *The Essential I Ching: The Oracle, Concise and to the Point*, 2012; Kindle edition

Bhaiji, *Matri Darshan (Mother as Revealed to Me)* (translation), revised edition 2004; Haridwar, India; Shree Shree Anandamayee Sangha

Blamires, Steve, *The Irish Celtic Magical Tradition*, 2012; Cheltenham, England; Skylight Press

Boram-Hays, Carol, "Borders of Beads: Questions of Identity in the Beadwork of the Zulu-Speaking People," 2005; *African Arts* 38, no. 2, pp 38–93

Briggs, Philip, and Chris McIntyre, *Northern Tanzania: Serengeti, Kilimanjaro, Zanzibar: the Bradt Travel Guide*, 2013; Chalfont St. Peter, England; Bradt Travel Guides

Chipasula, Frank Mkalawile (editor), *Bending the Bow: An Anthology of African Love Poetry*, 2009; Carbondale, Illinois; Southern Illinois University Press

Conway, D.J., *Celtic Magic: Llewellyn's World Magic Series*, 1990; Woodbury, Minnesota; Llewellyn Publications

Crichton, Jennifer, *Family Reunion: Everything You Need to Know to Plan Unforgettable Get-Togethers for Every Kind of Family*, 1998; New York; Workman Publishing

Cunningham, Scott, *Cunningham's Encyclopedia of Crystal, Gem and Metal Magic*, 2011; Woodbury, Minnesota: Llewellyn Publications

de Biasi, Jean-Louis, *The Magical Use of Prayer Beads: Secret Meditations & Rituals for Your Qabalistic, Hermetic, Wiccan or Druid Practice*, 2016; Woodbury, Minnesota; Llewellyn Publications

Dean, Bradley P. (editor), *Faith in a Seed: The Dispersion of Seeds and Other Late Natural History Writings*, 1993; Washington, DC; Shearwater Books, Island Press

Eliade, Mircea, *Shamanism: Archaic Techniques of Ecstasy*, 2004; Princeton, New Jersey; Princeton University Press

Evangelinos, Arēs, *The Komboloi and its History*, 1998; Nafplio, Greece; Komboloi Museum

Gillow, John, *African Textiles*, 2003; San Francisco; Chronicle Books

Gray, Henry, and Susannah Marriott, *Beads of Faith*, 2002; London; Carroll & Brown Publishers

Greer, John M., *The Celtic Golden Dawn: An Original & Complete Curriculum of Druidical Study*, 2013; Woodbury, Minnesota; Llewellyn Publications

Greer, John Michael, and Clare Vaughn, *Pagan Prayer Beads: Magic and Meditation with Pagan Rosaries*, 2007; San Francisco; Weiser

Harmer, Lucy, and Pip Waller, *Discovering Your Spirit Animal: The Wisdom of the Shamans*, 2009; Berkeley, California; North Atlantic Books

Harvey, Graham, and Robert J. Wallis, *Historical Dictionary of Shamanism*, 2016; Lanham, Maryland; Rowman & Littlefield

Hollis, Sir Alfred Claud, *The Masai: Their Language and Folklore*, 1905; Oxford, England; The Clarendon Press

Holmes, Emily A., Chris R. Brewin, and Richard G. Hennessy, "Trauma Films, Information Processing, and Intrusive Memory Development," 2004; *Journal of Experimental Psychology*, Volume 133, no. 1, pp 3–22

Kabat-Zinn, Jon, *Full Catastrophe Living: Using the Wisdom of Your Body and Mind to Face Stress, Pain, and Illness*, 2013; New York; Bantam Books

Kunz, George Frederick, *The Curious Lore of Precious Stones*, 1913; Philadelphia; J.B. Lippincott

Legge, James (translator), *Tao Te Ching*, 1891, in Volume 39 of Sacred Books of the East series, part II of The Texts of Confucianism; Oxford, England; The Clarendon Press; available at sacred-texts.com

Legge, James (translator), *The Yî King*, 1882, in Volume 16 of Sacred Books of the East series, part II of The Texts of Confucianism; Oxford, England; The Clarendon Press; available at sacred-texts.com

Lembo, Margaret Ann, *The Essential Guide to Crystals and Minerals*, 2013; Woodbury, Minnesota; Llewellyn Worldwide

Li, Feifei, Jianqin Li, Bo Liu, Jingxian Zhuo, and Chunlin Long, "Seeds used for Bodhi beads in China," 2014; *Journal of Ethnobiology and Ethnomedicine*

MacLeod, Sharon P., *Celtic Myth and Religion: A Study of Traditional Belief, with Newly Translated Prayers, Poems, and Songs*, 2012; Jefferson, North Carolina; McFarland & Company, Inc.

McCoy, Edain, *Celtic Myth & Magick: Harness the Power of the Gods and Goddesses*, 1995; Woodbury, Minnesota; Llewellyn Publications

Menjivar, Mark, *The Luck Archive: Exploring Belief, Superstition, and Tradition*, 2015; San Antonio, Texas; Trinity University Press

Netton, Ian Richard, *Encyclopedia of Islamic Civilisation and Religion*, 2010; London; Routledge

Peek, Philip M., and Kwesi Yankah, *African Folklore: An Encyclopedia*, 2009; London; Routledge

Permutt, Philip, *The Crystal Healer: Crystal Prescriptions That Will Change Your Life Forever*, 2016; London; CICO Books

Polk, Patti, *The Crystal Guide: Identification, Purpose, Powers and Values*, 2016; Iola, Wisconsin; Krause Publications, a division of F+W Media, Inc.

Prévert, Jacques, *Paroles*, 1958; San Francisco: City Lights Publishers

Quadrupani, Carlo Giuseppe, *Light and Peace: Instructions for Devout Souls to Dispel Their Doubts and Allay Their Fears*, 8th edition, 1918; St. Louis; B. Herder

Redgrove, H. Stanley, *Roger Bacon, the Father of Experimental Science and Mediæval Occultism*, 1920; London; W. Rider & Son

Russell, George William, *The Candle of Vision*, 1918; London; Macmillan and Co.

Ryan, M.J., (editor), *A Grateful Heart: Daily Blessings for the Evening Meal from Buddha to the Beatles*, 1994; Berkeley, California; Conari Press

Scully, Nicki, *Power Animal Meditations: Shamanic Journeys with Your Spirit Allies*, 2001; Rochester, Vermont; Bear & Co.

Shaku, Soyen, *Zen for Americans*, 1906; New York; Dorset Press; available at sacred-texts.com

Storl, Wolf-Dieter, PhD, *Shiva: The Wild God of Power and Ecstasy*, 2004; Rochester, Vermont; Inner Traditions

Suzuki, Daisetz T., *Zen and Japanese Culture*, 1959; Princeton, New Jersey; Bollingen Foundation, Inc.

Suzuki, Daisetz T., *Manual of Zen Buddhism*, 1935; available at sacred-texts.com

Taylor, Bron R. (editor), *Encyclopedia of Religion and Nature*, 2006 (online 2010); New York; Continuum

Tenzin Gyatso, Dalai Lama, "On the Meaning of: Om Mani Padme Hum"; available at sacred-texts.com

Tomalin, Stefany, *Beads: A History and Collector's Guide*, 2016; Stroud, England; Amberley Publishing

Tutu, Desmond, *No Future Without Forgiveness*, 2000; New York; Doubleday

Vincent, Kristen E., *A Bead and a Prayer: A Beginner's Guide to Protestant Prayer Beads*, 2013; Nashville, Tennessee; Upper Room Books

Wauters, Ambika, *The Complete Guide to Chakras: Unleash the Positive Power Within*, 2010; Hauppauge, NY; Barron's Publishing

Wiley, Eleanor, and Maggie Oman Shannon, *A String and a Prayer: How to Make and Use Prayer Beads*, 2002; San Francisco; Weiser

Willsher, Kim, "Click, Click: Komboloi Comeback as Stressed Greeks Rediscover Worry Beads," December 30, 2015; London; The *Guardian*

Winston, Kimberly, *Bead One, Pray Too: A Guide to Making and Using Prayer Beads*, 2008; New York; Morehouse Publishing

Yeats, William Butler, *The Celtic Twilight*, 2nd edition 1902; London; A.H. Bullen

websites

99namesofallah.name: list of the 99 names of Allah (Al Asma Ul Husna) with meaning and explanation

animalspirits.com: shamanism, working with animal spirits

anthromuseum.missouri.edu/minigalleries/prayerbeads/intros.html: "Prayer Beads: a cultural experience," Museum of Anthropology, College of Arts and Science, University of Missouri, 2015

Anthropos.eu: Father Mayr's "Zulu Proverbs," 1912; *Anthropos* Volume 7, no. 4, pp 957–63

bcponline.org: Book of Common Prayer

bluegecko.org/kenya/tribes/maasai/beliefs.htm: Jens Finke's "Maasai religion and beliefs—Traditional Music & Cultures of Kenya"

catholicculture.org/culture/library/view.cfm?recnum=5855: John Stokes, co-founder of Mary's Gardens, on naming flowers for Mary, mother of Jesus

catholictradition.org/Saints/signs4.htm: Pauly Fongemie's "Signs and Symbols Representing God and Saints: Plants, Trees, and Flowers"

chanttherosary.com/appendices/rosary-parts: Richard Poe, parts of the rosary

ctext.org/book-of-changes/yi-jing: Donald Sturgeon's contribution to the Chinese Text Project, on I Ching

discovered.us/stories/108/the-story-behind-maasai-beaded-jewelry-il-ngwesi

goodlucksymbols.com/bees: symbolism, superstition, and meaning of bees

greece.greekreporter.com/2012/12/05: Stella Tsolakidou's history of komboloi

kombologadiko.gr/historyen.html: discovering the enchanting world of the komboloi

maasai-association.org/art.html: "Maasai Art by Maasai is on view in U.S.A."

npr.org: National Public Radio's 2013 program "Ancient Beads with an Otherworldly Origin" with Ira Flatow and Thilo Rehren, PhD

poetryintranslation.com: A.S. Kline's translations of classic poetry, including *Ovid: The Love Poems New, Complete English Translations of The Amores, Ars Amatoria and Remedia Amoris*, 2015

sacred-texts.com: internet sacred text archive

sciencenetlinks.com/science-news/science-updates/worry-beads: Bob Hirshon and Emily Holmes on "Worry Beads"

shirleysafricancurios.com/beadwork.html

spectrumsca.com: Netanel Miles-Yépez, "The Day of the Dead in Mexican Culture," 2015; from online magazine *Delumin/a*

theconversation.com: Katherine Isbister's "Fidget toys aren't just hype"

tokenrock.com/explain-vision-quest-167.html: "Vision Quest—A Thorough Explanation"

zulubeadculture.weebly.com/symbols-and-meanings.html

resources

The best sources for materials are old jewelry boxes, your grandmother's drawer, and thrift shops, but there's a wonderful world of beads and supplies out there and the internet makes them all easily accessible. Some of the places I drew on for this book include:

BEADS OF PARADISE

beadsofparadisenyc.com

Beads of Paradise is a magical place! Filled with every bead imaginable from all reaches of the globe, it's a museum, educational resource, and shop all in one. The staff are knowledgeable and patient and their website is as inspiring as the bricks-and-mortar store.

FIRE MOUNTAIN GEMS

www.firemountaingems.com

Not only can you find an abundance of beads, their resources page also provides comprehensive and clear information about everything from varieties of glue to types of string, and even a handy beads-per-inch chart.

AFRICA DAVE

stores.ebay.com/africadave123

I stumbled upon Africa Dave's shop on eBay and returned several times. I was pleased by the quality and price of the beads (especially those from Ghana) and the speedy delivery.

LUCKY MOJO CURIO COMPANY

www.luckymojo.com

If I ever find myself in Forestville, California, the Lucky Mojo Company will be my first stop! You can while away the hours on their intriguing website and they sell every type of charm and amulet you could ever want—from the zany to the divine—all carefully curated.

MANY HANDS FARM

manyhandsfarm.weebly.com

When I was trying (and failing) to make rose-petal beads, I ordered some from Many Hands Farm so I would have a tangible model and not just a recipe. The beads were beautifully crafted and thoughtfully packaged and their rose petals some of the loveliest I've ever smelled.

I'm a big fan of improvising and finding the material that works best for you, but two products I've grown quite dependent on are Stretch Magic elastic cord and Beadalon silk cord (which comes in many widths and colors and with considerably pre-threaded needles).

Additional resources

US	UK
Artbeads **artbeads.com**	Burhouse **burhousebeads.com**
Beadalon **beadalon.com**	Cooksongold **cooksongold.com**
Bead for Life **beadforlife.org**	Creative Beadcraft **creativebeadcraft.co.uk**
Joann **joann.com**	Hobbycraft **hobbycraft.co.uk**
Michaels **michaels.com**	John Lewis **johnlewis.com**

index

acknowledgments

Many thanks to Carmel Edmonds, Cindy Richards, Kristine Pidkameny, Marion Paull, and all the talented and lovely people at CICO Books. Huge gratitude as well to William and Elsie Peck for their insights, Susan Lee Cohen for all her support, and Duane Stapp for his artistic perspective and patience.

photography credits

Photography is by Joanna Henderson and © CICO Books, except as listed below:

© CICO Books:

Geoff Dann: pages 11, 15, and 16

Kim Lightbody: page 33 (second from top)

David Merewether: pages 28, 63 (center right), and 96

Roy Palmer: pages 26, 27, 58, and 67

Edina van der Wyck: page 20

© Ryland Peters and Small:

Caroline Arber: page 54

Georgia Glynn-Smith: pages 33 (second from bottom) and 56

Caroline Hughes: page 33 (bottom)

Erin Kunkel: page 42

Paul Massey: page 114 (top) (thanks to www.janconstantine.com)

Debi Treloar: page 33 (top)

Chris Tubbs: page 63 (left, center left, and right)

© Getty Images:

ac productions: page 48

Arti Agarwal: page 97

Dirk Heuer: page 114

Jose Luiz Pelaez Inc.: page 41

Lane Oatey/Blue Jean Images: page 87

Steve Outram: page 108

John Seaton Callahan: page 91

Thomas Spencer/EyeEm: page 79

trinetuzun: page 66